AQ

ation

in

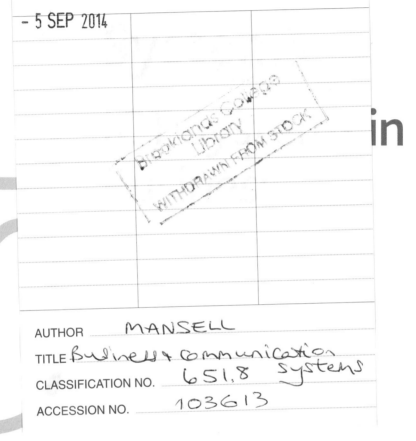
Diane Mansell
Kathryn Taylor

Series editor

Tim Chapman

rnes

Published in 2009 by:
Nelson Thornes Ltd
Delta Place
27 Bath Road
CHELTENHAM
GL53 7TH
United Kingdom

09 10 11 12 13 / 10 9 8 7 6 5 4 3 2 1

A catalogue record for this book is available from the British Library

ISBN 978 1 4085 0432 1

Cover photograph: John Birdsall
Illustrations by eMC Design Ltd

Page make-up by eMC Design Ltd, www.emcdesign.org.uk

Printed and bound in Spain by GraphyCems

Acknowledgements

The authors and publishers wish to thank the following for permission to use copyright
material:

p6 Keith Morris/Alamy; CO1 Marks & Spencer; page 8, Stoke City Football Club for an
extract from its 'Customer Charter'; 1.1A Getty Images; 1.1C Handypix/Alamy; 1.3A John
Lewis; 1.3B Marks & Spencer; CO2 Jupiter Images/BananaStock/Alamy; 2.1A eStock
Photo/Alamy; 2.2A Claude Thibault/Alamy; 2.3C Trinity Mirror/Mirrorpix/Alamy; 2.4A EDAW
Consortium/Handout/Reuters/Corbis; CO3 and 3.1A iStockphoto; 3.2A iStockphoto;
3.3A Ace Stock Limited/Alamy; 3.3B Image Source Pink/Alamy; 3.3C Bubbles Photo
Library/Alamy; 3.4A Dennis MacDonald/Alamy; 3.5B iStockphoto; 3.6A iStockphoto;
CO4 M. Timothy O'Keefe/Alamy; 4.1B Positive Image/Alamy; 4.1C iStockphoto; 4.1D
iStockphoto; 4.1G iStockphoto; 4.1H iStockphoto; 4.1I Fotolia; 4.2A Guy Primo/Alamy;
4.3A PSL Images/Alamy; 4.3B Gary Kucken/Alamy; 4.3C Alex Segre/Alamy; CO5 Nelson
Thornes; Ty Newydd Country Hotel; 5.4A iStockphoto; CO6 iStockphoto; 6.2A John Lewis;
6.3B Javier Larrea/Photolibrary; 6.3C Images of Birmingham/Alamy; 6.3D iStockphoto;
CO7 MIXA Co. Ltd/Alamy; 7.2B Paul Doyle/Alamy; 7.4B Michael Willis/Alamy; CO8
Comstock Images; 8.1A iStockphoto; 8.2B Ace Stock Limited/Alamy; 8.2C OJO Images
Limited/Alamy; 8.2D Alex Kamintzis; 8.3B Fotolia; 8.3C Mikael Karlsson/Alamy; 8.4C
Helene Rogers/Alamy; 8.4D Alex Kamintzis; CO9 Fancy/Veer/Corbis; C9 banner Sonny
Meddle/Rex Features; 9.1A Game Stores Group Ltd for material from its website; 9.2B
Go Education plc for material from the Go Projectors website; pages 94 and 95, QVC
for extracts from its 'Privacy Statement' and 'Returns Policy'; 9.3C First Direct; 9.3D
iStockphoto (both); page 100 iStockphoto (all).

Every effort has been made to contact the copyright holders and we apologise if any
have been overlooked. Should copyright have been unwittingly infringed in this book,
the owners should contact the publishers, who will make corrections at reprint.

Contents

Introduction		5
1	**The business environment**	**7**
1.1	Aims and objectives of business	8
1.2	What is a successful business?	10
1.3	Stakeholders	12
2	**Business administration**	**15**
2.1	What is administration?	16
2.2	Business functions	18
2.3	Roles and responsibilities	20
2.4	Planning and prioritising	22
3	**The workplace**	**25**
3.1	The working environment	26
3.2	Effective workplace design	28
3.3	Health and safety at work	30
3.4	Modern developments in work practices	32
3.5	Flexible working	34
3.6	Using resources with consideration	36
4	**Security of data**	**39**
4.1	ICT data systems in business	40
4.2	Methods of protecting data	44
4.3	Data protection and the law	46
5	**Recruitment and selection of staff**	**49**
5.1	Contract of employment	50
5.2	How to recruit the right person for the job	52
5.3	Selecting the best candidate	54
5.4	Employment rights and responsibilities	56

6 **Training and rewarding staff** **59**

6.1   Methods of training employees   60

6.2   Ways of paying staff   62

6.3   Rewards other than pay   64

7 **Communication** **67**

7.1   The purpose and importance of communication 68

7.2   Communication systems   70

7.3   Choosing the right medium   72

7.4   Barriers to communication   74

8 **ICT and business communications** **77**

8.1   Word processing   78

8.2   Spreadsheets   80

8.3   Databases   82

8.4   Graphics and desktop publishing   84

8.5   Using local and wide area networks   86

9 **The internet and e-commerce** **89**

9.1   The purpose of a website   90

9.2   Opportunities provided by having a website   92

9.3   Risks in using the internet   94

Examination-style questions   97

Index   102

Nelson Thornes has worked in partnership with AQA to ensure this book and the accompanying online resources offer you the best support for your GCSE course.

All resources have been approved by senior AQA examiners so you can feel assured that they closely match the specification for this subject and provide you with everything you need to prepare successfully for your exams.

These print and online resources together **unlock blended learning**; this means that between the activities in the book and the activities online you will maximise your understanding of a topic and help you achieve your potential.

These online resources are available on **kerboodle!** which can be accessed via the internet at www.kerboodle.com/live, anytime, anywhere. If your school or college subscribes to **kerboodle!** you will be provided with your own personal login details. Once logged in, access your course and locate the required activity.

For more information and help on how to use **kerboodle!** visit www.kerboodle.com.

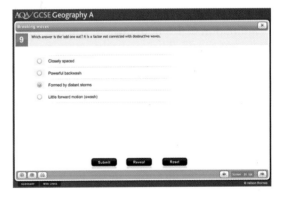

How to use this book

Objectives

Look for the list of **Learning Objectives** based on the requirements of this course so you can ensure you are covering everything you need to know for the exam.

AQA Examiner's tip

Don't forget to read the **AQA Examiner's Tips** throughout the book as well as practise answering **Examination-style Questions**.

Visit www.nelsonthornes.com/aqagcse for more information.

AQA examination-style questions are reproduced by permission of the Assessment and Qualifications Alliance.

GCSE Business and Communication Systems

GCSE Business and Communication Systems is one of the courses on offer from the AQA Business Subjects and Economics Specification.

In this course you will learn about:

- the environment in which a business operates and how it affects the success of the business
- how administrative work supports all the other parts of the business
- the way the workplace can be organised so that people can do their jobs effectively and safely
- how ICT data is managed and kept secure
- how people are recruited, trained and rewarded for their work and the rights they have
- the purpose of communication and why it is so important to a business
- the importance of the internet and e-commerce
- how to choose appropriate software applications for specific business tasks, such as web authoring or creating spreadsheets
- investigating how ICT is used in a real business environment.

There are three examined units:

Unit 8 ICT Systems in Business – written paper of 1 hour based on the content of this book.

Unit 9 Using ICT in Business – you will be assessed by computer-based examination of 1.5 hours where you use your practical ICT skills to carry out specific business tasks.

Unit 10 Investigating ICT in Business – Controlled Assessment, where you use your skills and knowledge from Unit 9 to investigate the use of ICT beyond the classroom.

What is this book about?

This book covers all you need to know for the Unit 8 examination and mirrors the Specification exactly. Each chapter has an introduction outlining what you will learn and is split into topics. Within each topic, clear learning objectives are provided that relate directly to what you will need to know and key terms are defined. Each topic uses examples you can relate to. The activities will enable you to check your learning and apply it to new questions. The chapters have summary questions at the end that will enable your to check your knowledge and understanding of the content of the whole chapter.

The book also contains examination-style questions written in a way you may expect in your final examination. This part of the book is intended to demystify the examination and give you the skills and knowledge to enter the examination with confidence.

Units 9 and 10 will be covered by online resources on **kerboodle!** and your teacher will direct you to these to help you complete the course.

1 The business environment

In this chapter

1.1	Aims and objectives of business
1.2	What is a successful business?
1.3	Stakeholders

This chapter looks at the environment that businesses work in. It will introduce you to what a business might aim to achieve and the groups of people who might be affected by the action of a business.

You will consider what aims and objectives a business might have and to understand that not all businesses have the same objectives.

Real business examples are used to show how aims and objectives vary between businesses. You will see that a business making knitwear will have very different objectives to a football team.

Business success can be judged in several ways and the success of a business can be measured by how far it has achieved its objectives. For some businesses success might be large profits, but others might choose to judge their success in different ways. Issues such as business ethics are becoming much more important to some businesses than making ever-bigger profits.

You will learn who may be a stakeholder in a business and understand that stakeholders have different interests that might compete with each other. A stakeholder such as an employee might want different things from the business than the owner, who is also a stakeholder. A business must try to keep all of its stakeholders happy with its activities.

An **aim** is a 'big idea' about what a business wants to achieve. John Smedley Knitwear is a business based in Derbyshire which has been producing very high-quality knitwear for over 200 years. It might aim to be known as one of the best knitwear manufacturers in the world. Stoke City Football Club, on the other hand, might aim to retain its place in the Premier League. (It was promoted at the end of the 2007–2008 season.) Another of its aims is shown here from its website.

Objectives

In order to achieve their aims, businesses must set a number of **objectives**. These are targets that will clearly state what the business wants to achieve. Setting objectives helps everyone in the business to be clear about what they are trying to achieve. People will be working towards the same goals. Many of us will think that the most important objective of all businesses is to make as much profit as possible. Other objectives are also important.

Some business objectives are set to meet short-term goals such as reducing the amount of money spent on telephone calls this year. Other objectives are set to cover long-term targets such as Marks & Spencer's target of sending no waste to landfill sites by 2012.

> 66 *Stoke City FC aims to provide the best standards of service to supporters in relation to all its activities.* 99
>
> **www.stokecityfc.com**

Survival

When a business is first set up, the owners will want it to survive. Many businesses do not make it past the first year, so survival is an obvious objective for a new business. In order to survive, the business will hope to break even. This means that the money they receive from their customers matches the money they have spent running the business. John Smedley Knitwear and Stoke City FC are both well-established businesses, so survival will not necessarily be an objective.

Key terms

Aim: a broad statement of what a business would like to achieve over a longer period of time.

Objective: a specific target for a business to meet, which helps them to achieve their overall aim(s).

AQA *Examiner's tip*

Do not always assume that profit is the main objective of all businesses. Look carefully at the business in the question.

A *A supporter of Stoke City FC*

Profit

All businesses need to make a **profit**. In the long term, without profits they cannot continue to trade as the business is spending more than it is receiving. Some businesses are famous for the huge amounts of profits they make. For example, in 2007 Tesco made over £2.8 billion profits. Profit is important as the money made can be put back into the business to help it to achieve other objectives. Stoke City FC can use profits to buy better players.

Growth

A business might have the objective of growing in size and the profits it makes can help to achieve this. A growing business can buy new machinery, employ more people or buy more goods to sell. John Smedley Knitwear has grown over its long history. As more of its products are sold, it can use profits to increase the size of its factory and buy more technologically advanced knitting machines. Many businesses might have growth as an objective as it could result in more sales and profits.

Reputation and image

John Smedley Knitwear has built up a reputation over the years for selling very high-quality products. Its knitwear is popular with celebrities and is regularly featured in fashion magazines. It has a fashionable and upmarket image. The behaviour of Stoke City FC's players off the pitch could improve or spoil the image of the club.

Possible objectives for John Smedley Knitwear

- Increase sales by 5 per cent this year.
- Feature in at least three fashion magazines this year.
- Cut costs by 1 per cent in the factory.

Possible objectives for Stoke City FC

- Finish the season in the top ten of the Premier League.
- Increase ticket sales at home games.
- Reduce queuing time for fans at food outlets during matches.

Key terms

Profit: the difference between the money a business receives from selling and the money it spends on running the business.

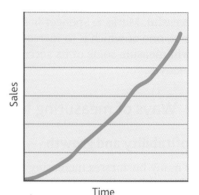

B *Graph showing sales rising*

C *John Smedley Knitwear has a very good reputation*

Activities

1 In groups consider what aims and objectives the following businesses might have:

Business	Aims	Objectives
Budget airline		
House builder		
Mobile phone manufacturer		
International confectionery manufacturer		
A national radio station		

2 Use the internet to find out the latest profit figures for these businesses and some others you are interested in:

- Manchester United FC
- Marks & Spencer
- ITV.

Which makes the most profit? What image do they have? Are they still growing? How long have they survived?

What is a successful business?

A successful business is one that meets its objectives. Objectives can cover a wide range of business activity so there are many different ways of deciding if a business is successful. If one of Tesco's objectives for 2007 was to make profits of over £2 billion, then it has been very successful. Marks & Spencer has many objectives related to reducing waste, one of which is to increase the number of coat hangers it reuses. It will measure some of its success by how far it has achieved these objectives.

Objectives

Understand that business success can be judged in several ways.

Understand that the success of a business links to how far it has achieved its objectives.

Ways of measuring business success

Profitability and growth

For many businesses increasing their profits (i.e. being more profitable) each year is an important measure of their success. Without profits it is difficult for a business to grow. Growth can be measured by increases in profits or sales. Ryanair has seen its profitability fall in 2008 due to the high cost of fuel. However, Westfield, the shopping mall developer, continues to grow. It opened a huge new mall in West London in 2008, and has more planned for Bradford in 2010 and Stratford, East London, which is close to the Olympic site, in 2011. Many businesses have been able to use the internet to help increase their sales and profits. Many well-known high-street retailers now also sell through websites.

Key terms

Growth: the increase in size of a business's sales or profits.

Profitability: the ability of a business to make profits.

Market share: the amount of sales a business has compared to the whole market, usually expressed as a percentage.

Activities

1 Find out the most up-to-date profit figures for Coca-Cola, Microsoft and McDonald's (three of the biggest businesses in the world). In how many different ways could these businesses be viewed as successful?

2 Research your local town or city and find out the following:

a Which businesses are the most successful?

b How are you judging this success?

c Which businesses are creating new jobs?

d What sort of jobs are they?

e Do any of the local businesses put ethical values ahead of profits?

   Present your findings as a word-processed report or as a presentation using a suitable software package.

Market share

Tesco has the biggest share of UK supermarket sales. This is another way to judge its success. This means that its sales are bigger than any other supermarket rival.

For many businesses, having the biggest share of their market is an important measure of their success. It could mean that they can have more influence over prices in their market.

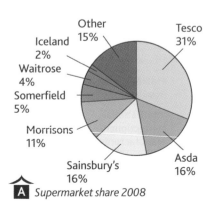

A *Supermarket share 2008*

Job creation

If a business grows it will need to employ more people. This is an important measure of success as the local community and the whole country benefit if new jobs are created. This is because people will earn wages which they might then spend in local shops and businesses. The country benefits because employees pay taxes to the government from their wages. The new Westfield shopping malls will create many new jobs.

Insulation firms set for growth and job creation

By Anna Blackaby, Business Staff

Hundreds of jobs look set to be created in the Midlands as insulation firms reap the benefits of the Government's energy efficiency drive for homes.

Leicester-based energy efficiency firm Mark Group said it was creating 115 jobs in Birmingham in the coming year under plans to open a new distribution hub in the city.

The Birmingham Post, *12 September 2008*

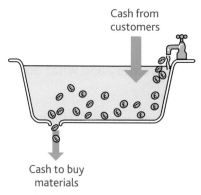

Cash from customers

Cash to buy materials

 Cash flowing out of a business to buy materials before cash flows in from customers

Cash flow

Cash is not the same as profit. Many successful businesses make a profit by selling their goods or services for more than they cost to produce. However, cash is needed to buy materials, pay wages and bills, often before the business receives any money from their customers. Making sure that enough cash is flowing into the business is an important measure of their success. A house builder could face **cash flow** problems as a great deal of money must be spent on materials many months, or even years, before they receive any cash from customers from sales. On the other hand, a shop on the High Street might have fewer cash flow problems as their customers pay as soon as they make a purchase.

Ethics

Ethics are values and principles that a business believes are important. They might believe that these values are more important than making large profits. Ethics often cover areas such as fair trade, reducing waste and treating workers fairly. The online fashion shop People Tree aims to sell clothing that is traded fairly and which has as little impact on the environment as possible.

People Tree will judge some of its success by whether it has met its ethical aims. Marks & Spencer has Plan A, which is its five-year, ten-point plan to tackle a wide range of issues such as reducing waste and recycling more. More businesses are now measuring their success in these ethical terms as well as the traditional measures such as profits and growth.

> **Key terms**
>
> **Cash flow:** the amount of money flowing into the business from selling, and flowing out to buy materials and pay bills.
>
> **Ethics:** principles and values that influence how a business is run.

> **AQA Examiner's tip**
>
> Do not confuse cash with profits. A business can be profitable but still run out of cash.

> 66 *To supply customers with good quality products, with friendly and efficient service and build awareness to empower consumers and producers to participate in Fair Trade and environmentally sustainable solutions.* 99
>
> *www.peopletree.co.uk*

1.3 Stakeholders

What is a stakeholder?

A **stakeholder** is a person or group of people who are interested in how successful the business is. Some stakeholders might believe that what they want is more important than another stakeholder.

Who are they and what do they want?

Owners

The people who own a business will have invested their own money into the business. Their reward for this is a share of the profits. The owners of large businesses are called shareholders and often do not have anything to do with the business on a day-to-day basis. The shareholders in Marks & Spencer will be happy as the business made over £1 billion profit in 2008 for the first time in 11 years. Because they have invested some of their money into the business, they expect a share of the profits and will, therefore, want the business to make as much profit as possible.

Employees

People who work for a business expect to be paid a reasonable wage (at least the minimum wage or better). **Trade unions** work to protect employees from being treated unfairly. For example, unions campaigned to get the government to agree that tips paid to waiters and waitresses could not be included as part of their minimum-wage hourly pay. Employees also hope to work in a pleasant and comfortable environment and to be treated fairly. This adds to business costs and, therefore, reduces profits. So what an employee wants could be in conflict with what the owners want.

Customers

When customers buy something from a shop they expect that it will be of good quality. However, some businesses might find the cheapest place to buy their goods to keep their costs down and their profits up. This can affect the quality of the goods sold.

Customers also want good service. Employees are the people who provide this service. The way that they deal with customers can have a big impact on the image and reputation of the business. Boden, the clothing retailer, frequently sends out online questionnaires to collect feedback from its customers. Happy employees are more likely to keep customers happy. This might sometimes cost more to offer but usually pays for itself with customer loyalty.

Local people

A business can have a very positive impact on a town or city. In 2009 John Lewis opened a store in Cardiff. The development will have cost £500 million. This will bring many new jobs to the city for the developers and shop staff and, perhaps, more custom for other nearby shops. Some local people might be unhappy at the thought of more traffic and crowds coming into the city or be concerned that other stores could lose custom because of the new John Lewis development.

A *The John Lewis development St David's, Cardiff*

The government

The government wants businesses to be successful because businesses create wealth. This means that the money people earn and then spend in shops, cafés and the like helps other businesses to be successful. The government will help and encourage businesses but they pass **legislation** to make sure that businesses behave responsibly. There is legislation covering things such as:

- the minimum wage workers should be paid
- health and safety at work
- reducing waste and increasing recycling.

The environment

The government is taking a bigger role in looking after the environment. It has introduced legislation to protect the environment from being spoilt by business activity. **Sustainability** influences the way many businesses operate. Indigo Furniture based in Matlock uses reclaimed and sustainable timber to make its products and works in partnership with the Woodland Trust. Responsible Travel (**www.responsibletravel.com**) offers holidays that respect the environment and local people.

Can everyone be happy?

Ashbourne is a small market town on the edge of the Peak District, with a population of about 7,000 people. Cedar House Investments has developed a small edge-of-town business park called Waterside Park. So far Homebase, Halfords and Selecta Tyre have established themselves there. In the autumn of 2008, Marks & Spencer applied for permission for a change of use for one of the empty units, so that it can open a Marks & Spencer Simply Food outlet. The proposal has been met with widely differing views from various stakeholders. Many local shoppers welcome the news as it increases the choice of shops, whereas some of the independent local retailers, which include three butchers, a fishmonger, a greengrocer, a delicatessen and several florists, have different views.

The business park is on land that once was home to a Nestlé factory which was not very attractive. For more information on this go to **www.bbc.co.uk** and use its search engine to find the article 'Changing Ashbourne – the Nestlé factory site'.

B   *Marks & Spencer applied for permission to open a Simply Food outlet at Waterside Park*

Case study

1

In this chapter you have learnt:

✔ what business aims and objectives are and why setting them helps a business to achieve its goals

✔ that a successful business is not always the one with the highest profits. Success is measured in several ways

✔ who the different stakeholders in a business might be and how they influence a business.

Revision question

Match the term to the correct definition:

Term	Definition
1 Ethics	**A** A specific target for a business to meet, which helps them to achieve their overall aim(s).
2 Cash flow	**B** An organisation that employees can join, which represents their interests.
3 Trade union	**C** Principles and values that influence how a business is run.
4 Profit	**D** The amount of sales a business has compared to the whole market, usually expressed as a percentage.
5 Objective	**E** The amount of money flowing into the business from selling, and flowing out to buy materials and pay bills.
6 Market share	**F** A broad statement of what a business would like to achieve over a longer period of time.
7 Aim	**G** A person or group with an interest in a business.
8 Stakeholder	**H** The difference between the money a business receives from selling and the money it spends on running the business.

Case study

Coca-Cola is one of the best-known businesses in the world. Its drinks are sold across the globe. It aims to earn as much profit as it can for its owners, but is aware of its responsibilities to its many stakeholders. See **www.thecoca-colacompany.com** and **www.cokecce.co.uk** for more information.

Activities

Answer the following questions:

1 State and explain three different ways in which Coca-Cola could be judged as a successful business.

2 Explain how these different stakeholders might influence Coca-Cola:

■ customers

■ employees

■ people who live near one of their bottling factories.

3 Which of Coca-Cola's many stakeholders do you think will have most power over the business? Justify your answer.

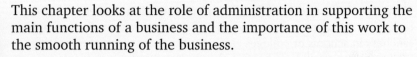

2 Business administration

In this chapter

2.1 What is administration?

2.2 Business functions

2.3 Roles and responsibilities

2.4 Planning and prioritising

This chapter looks at the role of administration in supporting the main functions of a business and the importance of this work to the smooth running of the business.

The first learning objectives are to understand what administration involves and the importance of having effective systems to prepare, store, process and retrieve information. The sort of system used will depend on the type of data being stored and used.

You will then learn what the main business functions are and how administration supports these functions. For example, if someone has an interview, the human resources department might conduct the interviews, but the role of administration is very important in making sure that all the application forms have been copied to the right people and that the candidates know where and when to arrive for interview.

The next unit will enable you to understand the features of hierarchical and flat business structures. Some businesses have more levels of management than others. You will learn that there are different job roles in a business and that some roles carry more responsibility than others. Managers have more responsibility than others and their work is less routine than someone whose job is to carry out administrative tasks.

You will then consider why planning is important and examine all the processes involved in effective planning. You will consider the importance of planning for a huge event such as the Olympic Games and, in contrast, the opening of a small shop. For both projects to be successful, effective planning is essential.

Many people carry out work called **administration**. It means that the tasks they do support the main work of an organisation. For example, teachers in schools or colleges carry out the main work of educating students. There will be other people employed to keep accurate records of student attendance which is used on reports and for official records. Others will be responsible for entering students for the correct GCSE and A Level examinations. Whatever their role, all these jobs will involve similar principles.

Data preparation and input

Businesses and organisations such as schools and hospitals acquire an enormous amount of **data**. Some members of the administration staff will need to prepare this data for use by others. This often means that they need to enter data into a database. Whenever a teacher takes an electronic register, they are inputting data into a system. Many hairdressers use an electronic appointment system, so the receptionist is inputting data into the system to organise the stylist's day. If the data is not entered completely accurately, the student could be wrongly accused of missing a lesson, or the client expecting a new hairstyle might find there is no record of their appointment.

Data storage

Imagine if all the paper was left to pile up day after day! Picture the inbox that was not checked frequently! An effective administration system will need a suitable way of storing all the data received and generated.

There are two broad ways of storing data:

- the traditional filing of paper in suitable cabinets, often known as a manual system
- by electronic storage.

Paper storage is suitable for:

- letters received
- copies of any document not produced by a computer, such as a birth certificate
- receipts which are proof of purchase.

Some of this can be stored elsewhere when it is old, but still needs to be kept safely. This is called archiving. Docusave, based in Surrey, runs an entire business offering data storage services. See **www.docusave.co.uk**.

Electronic storage is suitable for:

- any document sent or received electronically
- numerical data in a spreadsheet
- any records that can be held in a database, such as patients' details in a hospital.

A database is a powerful storage and processing tool which is looked at in more detail in Chapter 8.

Key terms

Administration: the tasks that support the main purpose of the business and ensure that it is run effectively.

Data: facts and figures of any sort held by a business that can be processed to give information.

A A receptionist in a hairdresser's uses an electronic booking system

AQA Examiner's tip

You might be asked to suggest suitable storage methods for some business data. Think about what sort of data is suitable for paper or electronic storage.

Electronically stored data must be backed up regularly, i.e. stored again on a single computer or on another storage device to ensure that the data is not lost. You will look at methods of protecting data in more detail in Chapter 4.

Whatever storage method is used, the input of the data must be accurate or it will be of little use to anyone else.

Data processing

Data is any sort of facts and figures that a business holds. It may be sales figures or wages paid, held on a spreadsheet, in student reports in a school or as any other kind of paper or electronic document. In its raw state, data is not necessarily very useful. A huge pile of paper does not immediately tell you anything useful. The administration team will make data more useful for the people who need it by **processing** it in some way. Processing data means that it is turned into information that is more meaningful.

Ways of processing data

- Sorting data alphabetically or numerically.
- Storing documents in order of receipt.
- Producing a summary of a long report.
- Using a database to search and sort the data (see Chapter 8).

Retrieval of information

Stored data needs to be easily accessible to the people who need it. No one wants to have to keep going to the archives (which may be several miles away from the main business site) to find a piece of paper. The storage method should suit the need to access the information. The electronic database is popular because it provides almost instant access to a huge amount of data, and can be protected from unauthorised use. Once data has been **retrieved** it can be **disseminated** to the right people. The administration team can ensure that the correct papers are prepared for a particular meeting.

Summary of an effective administration system

- Data is prepared accurately.
- Data is stored in an appropriate and secure way.
- Processing is carried out to make the data useful to the user.
- Data can be retrieved easily and be disseminated to those who need it.

Key terms

Data processing: dealing with data in a way that makes it more useful to the user – providing information.

Data retrieval: finding the data needed as quickly and simply as possible.

Disseminate: pass on data to those who need to use it.

Case study

The spreadsheet shows sales figures for 12 months for a business selling toys. Diagram **B** shows data in a spreadsheet and as a chart. Why is the data more useful when presented as a chart?

	A	B	C	D	E	F	G
1	Jan	300					
2	Feb	400					
3	Mar	500					
4	Apr	450					
5	May	400					
6	Jun	250					
7	Jul	200					
8	Aug	300					
9	Sep	375					
10	Oct	425					
11	Nov	495					
12	Dec	500					

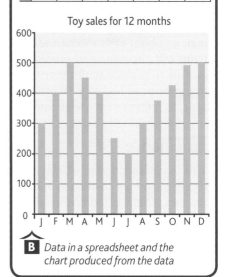

B Data in a spreadsheet and the chart produced from the data

Activities

1. Investigate the administration system at your school and college. Find out about how the following tasks are done and by whom.
   a Keeping data on student contact details.
   b Keeping records of student attendance.
   c Keeping data on student test results.
   d Dealing with lost property.
   e Organising the production of student reports.

2. Write a word-processed report for each task, outlining how data is prepared, processed and retrieved. Comment on how effective you think the administration systems are for these tasks.

You can learn more about administration by focusing on some of the key functions in a business. You will remember that administration supports the main purpose of the business, so we will look in more detail at this support. In a large business many people will work in one business function whereas in a small business one person might carry out several functions.

Human resources

The **human resources** (HR) function is responsible for recruiting, selecting, training and paying employees. If a branch of a large hotel needs a new chef, the administration team will make sure that the job is advertised in the right place on the right date. When the interviews are held the administration team will have contacted all the candidates so that they know what time to turn up for their interviews. They would expect to be sent directions and a map to show exactly where to go. The personal details and applications from each person will be stored appropriately and be retrieved and disseminated when they are needed.

Marketing and sales

The **marketing** function of a business covers all the activities that tell customers about the business and lead to an increase in sales. The Malmaison Hotel chain will market itself to customers by such things as advertising in glossy magazines and inviting journalists to write reviews about their rooms and food in newspapers. The administration team will also store and process sales data. For example, they will be able to provide senior managers with information about which branches have had more rooms booked than others. They might also provide information about competing hotels.

Finance

This business function will be concerned with the money the business receives from its customers and the amount it spends. At Gordon Ramsey Holdings, administrative teams will store and process this data. Reports can be prepared to show details such as how much money comes in from all its different restaurants and pubs. In a small one-person business, such as Guitars 4 You, a guitar retailer, the owner will carry out most of these functions himself. He produces all the advertising material himself, keeps all the accounts and deals individually with all the customers.

Customer services

The customer services function is very important as an unhappy customer might not use a business again and that customer could be lost to a competitor. In a shop like Marks & Spencer there is a separate counter for customer services where most enquiries and complaints can be dealt with. Apple can offer customer support on its website and through face-to-face contact in its stores. The Next Directory uses a telephone call centre as the way of dealing with customer queries. The administration team will support this function by making sure that customers' records are kept up to date and can be easily retrieved. The call centre operator will be able to deal with an angry customer more effectively if they have the correct information to hand.

Research and development

Apple is famous for its innovative products. It is constantly researching and developing new products. In 2007 it launched the iPod touch which has incredible features.

These products come from a great deal of work carried out by the **research and development** (R&D) staff. Administration is essential in supporting this work as data might be gathered and processed from market research to find out what customers want. Administrative teams can prepare presentations and reports for the product developer to tell them what customers do and do not like. This information helps Apple to keep ahead of its competitors.

A *Apple iPod touch*

Operations

The **operations** function is about making sure that products or services are delivered to customers when needed. It is also responsible for the quality of the goods and services it produces. Emma Bridgewater Pottery is made in a factory in Stoke-on-Trent. The factory is responsible for making sure that enough of each design is made and sent to the right places. A lot of administrative work will be involved in recording orders accurately, and processing the correct documents to show when orders have been despatched and paid for. The operations function in a catering business will make sure that all the food, staff and equipment are organised so that catering at an event runs smoothly. If the food runs out half way through a wedding, the operations function has not worked effectively.

The importance of good administrative support

- Helps all parts of the business to run smoothly.
- Supports the main business functions by keeping accurate data about sales, payments, customer satisfaction, employee records.
- The information provided by the data can help the business keep up to date with what customers want and compete with rival businesses.

2.3   Roles and responsibilities

Business structures

The people who work in a business need to be organised in some way. Usually they are organised into business functions as can be seen in Figure A. Within these functions there will be some jobs that carry more **responsibility** than others. Managers have more responsibility than others in the organisation and are 'higher up' the business organisation.

A Pyramid showing the levels of management in an organisation

(Pyramid labels: Senior Management, Middle Managers, Assistant Managers, Supervisors, Operatives)

Hierarchical structures

Some businesses have a 'tall' structure. The levels in the pyramid show who is responsible for whom.

A hierarchical structure usually has several layers, with more **authority** being held at the top of the **hierarchy**. Lower down, there will be **supervisors** who will have some responsibility delegated to them from senior managers. At the bottom, operatives have the least responsibility.

Flat structures

Some business structures have fewer levels of management and are therefore 'flatter' than those with lots of levels. This means that there are fewer middle managers and supervisors. Communication is easier in a flat structure as there are fewer 'levels' to go through. It can mean, though, that a manager has more people to manage than in a tall structure.

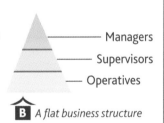

B A flat business structure

(Pyramid labels: Managers, Supervisors, Operatives)

Roles and responsibilities

Managers

Whether a business is 'flat' or 'hierarchical', there are fewer people at the top than the bottom. The managers at the top will make important, **non-routine decisions** that will affect the whole business. Managers are paid more than others because they take these important decisions and they carry the responsibility if they go wrong.

Examples of non-routine decisions

- Cadbury bringing back the Wispa bar in 2008.
- The Westfield Group planning shopping centres for 2009 and beyond.
- Nokia's decision to open its Music Store to compete with Apple's iTunes.

Objectives

Understand the features of hierarchical and flat business structures.

Understand the different job roles in a business and that some roles carry more responsibility than others.

Understand the difference between routine and non-routine tasks.

Key terms

Responsibility: having control over how a task is carried out and a duty to make sure it is done as well as possible.

Authority: someone with authority has a right to make a decision or perform a task.

Hierarchy: a business that has several layers of managers and supervisors from the top to the bottom.

Supervisor: someone who makes sure that other people are carrying out their job correctly and safely.

Non-routine decision: a decision that is taken less frequently, for example launching a new product.

AQA Examiner's tip

You might be asked to suggest who would carry out a particular task or make a certain decision in a business situation.

These sorts of decisions will affect the whole business so it is important that the people with the right skills take them. The quality of the information that is provided by people lower down the organisation will also affect these decisions.

For example, the decision to bring back the Wispa bar, which Cadbury first launched in the 1980s, will have been taken based on information gathered from customers. Those who know the chocolate market very well would then have finally made the decision.

C Cadbury decided to relaunch the Wispa bar

In a hierarchical structure there will be junior managers who will carry out more **routine decision** making.

Examples of routine decisions

- Working out the rota for staff breaks in a department store.
- Ordering new supplies of paper and printer cartridges as they are needed.

Supervisors and operatives

Supervisors usually manage a team of operatives. Operatives are the employees at the 'bottom' of the business structure. Their work usually is made up of **routine tasks**. For example, in a bank some people are employed to input data about people's accounts into a system. Many banks use call centres to deal with customers. Call centre operators will only be able to deal with routine tasks such as a customer calling to pay a bill from their bank account. However, someone calling because they believe money is being stolen from their account would most likely be passed on to a supervisor, as this is a **non-routine task**.

Activity

1   Using a business that you know or the school or college you attend, find out the following:

a   Find out about the structure of the business or school and sketch a diagram to show if it is flat or hierarchical.

b   Identify a manager and describe two non-routine decisions they might have to make.

c   Identify an employee who will carry out routine tasks. Describe what these tasks might be.

d   Describe the advantages and disadvantages of:
   i   being a manager
   ii being an operative.

Planning and prioritising

Planning

Businesses will **plan** for all sorts of things. The staff Christmas party, while not an essential business activity, needs to be planned if it is to be successful. Many employees have to decide in September what they will eat at the party in December. At the other end of the scale, imagine the level of planning involved to prepare for the Olympic Games in London in 2012!

A *London 2012, a huge planning exercise*

Key terms

Plan: a set of decisions about how to do something in the future.

Case study

Go to **www.london2012.com/plans** to find out about the huge amount of planning involved in delivering the 2012 Olympic Games. Why do you think that planning is so important in this case? What could be the consequence of poor planning?

The importance of planning

A well-planned event often runs so smoothly that no one realises that a great deal of work has taken place to achieve it. If an event is well planned it will have achieved its purpose and this reflects well on the organisers. Lakeland, the homeware retailer, is planning to open a branch in Derby. If this is planned properly, an attractive shop will open on time, with trained staff ready to serve the public. This will enable Lakeland to sell more of its products.

Successful planning

There are several steps to carry out if a plan is to be successful:

| 1 Identify all the tasks required. | → | 2 Work out how long each task should take. | → | 3 Decide the order in which the tasks should be done. | → | 4 Decide who will carry out each task. |

AQA Examiner's tip

You need to be able to apply the principles of planning to any situation. You might need to advise on how best to plan a given task.

Planning in practice

Leona is going to open a shop selling flowers. She has found suitable premises, but needs to plan for the opening so that everything will run smoothly and she will be ready to serve her first customers.

Identifying what needs to be done

Leona has scribbled down on paper what needs to be done and how many days before opening day they need to be done:

Order flowers to arrive day before opening	7 days
Decorator to paint shop	2 days
Order paper, ribbon etc. for bouquets	14 days
Arrange for shop fitter to put up shelves and fit counter	3 days
Arrange an advertisement in the local paper	7 days
Order shelving, counter, buckets etc. for display of flowers	21 days

Prioritising

Prioritising will make sure that everything is ready for the shop opening day. Leona must decide which tasks must be done before others. For example, it is important that the shop fitters have completed their work before the decorator arrives.

Leona rewrites the list with ordered and prioritised tasks.

1	Order shelving, counter etc.	21 days
2	Order paper, ribbon etc.	14 days
3	Order flowers	7 days
4	Place advertisement in paper	7 days
5	Shop fitter	3 days
6	Decorator	2 days

This list now helps Leona to see what she needs to do and what she must arrange for others to do. It also shows which tasks rely on each other being done first. The following steps are essential for effective planning:

- Work out what needs to be done.
- Decide how long each task will take.
- Prioritise the tasks.
- Give each task to the right person.
- Communicate with everyone involved in the task, so that they know the priorities and deadline.

Consequences of poor planning

The results of poor planning will depend on the nature of the task. If the planning for the opening of the new Lakeland store is poor, the opening could be delayed, leaving customers frustrated and affecting its reputation. If, for example, a meeting has not been planned properly, the consequences could be that:

- not everyone who should have been there attended
- not enough copies of documents were available
- the time ran out before everything on the agenda could be discussed
- the venue was unsuitable resulting in people not being able to see or hear a presentation.

Activity

Planning an event

1. Split into groups for this activity. In your group, choose one of the following events which you will produce a plan for:

   - a school ball
   - a day trip to Paris, including a visit to the Eiffel Tower
   - a talent show at your school or college.

   a Devise and document all the tasks that will need to be done.

   b Work out an order of priority and timing of each task.

   c Decide who will do each task.

   d Produce a final plan to present to your class explaining how you prioritised the tasks.

   e Ask for feedback. You might have forgotten something!

2

In this chapter you have learnt:

✔ the tasks that are involved in administration and how this supports the work of all the other business functions

✔ that those at the 'top' of a business have more responsibility and authority than those at the 'bottom'. The work of managers is usually less routine than the work of operatives lower down

✔ the importance of planning and what is needed for it to be effective, in order to avoid the consequences of poor planning.

Revision questions

1 Write a clear definition of the following terms, giving a business example to support your answer.

a Data

b Processing

c Responsibility

d Prioritising

e Hierarchy

f Non-routine decision

2 Parnham Parties was set up in Wilmslow, Cheshire, by a mother and daughter team, Anthea and Nicola Parnham. The business provides food for weddings and parties.

Nicola is the manager responsible for finance and marketing. She runs the office which employs an assistant manager, Mitul, and two assistants, Mary and Alan. Mitul has responsibility for the overall planning of an event and supervises the work of Alan and Mary. Alan keeps all the customer records and sends out bills to customers for their events. Mary is responsible for placing newspaper and magazine advertisements. She also books the venues for parties.

Anthea runs the operations side of the business. She prepares the food with Sue and Sarah. They also transport the food to the events and act as waitresses if needed. Anthea views Sue and Sarah as equal team members to her and they all share whatever jobs are needed to be done.

a Draw a pyramid diagram to show the structure of Nicola's part of the business. Explain your diagram.

b Explain one reason why Nicola's job is more difficult than Alan's or Mary's.

c Describe one advantage and one disadvantage of the way the operations side of the business is managed.

d Explain three ways in which Mitul's planning can make sure that the parties are successful.

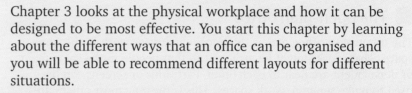

3 The workplace

In this chapter

3.1 The working environment

3.2 Effective workplace design

3.3 Health and safety at work

3.4 Modern developments in work practices

3.5 Flexible working

3.6 Using resources with consideration

Chapter 3 looks at the physical workplace and how it can be designed to be most effective. You start this chapter by learning about the different ways that an office can be organised and you will be able to recommend different layouts for different situations.

Following on from this you will learn about the importance of ergonomics, which is making sure that the furniture and equipment someone uses is suitable for their work. You will understand why considering health and safety at work is so important and why employers must provide a safe working environment. The increasing use of ICT at work means that more thought has to be given to how continued use of computers could affect someone's health.

New technology means that where and how people carry out their work is changing. You will learn about these new technologies, such as video conferencing, and be able to recommend when they might be used effectively. This means that people can work flexibly and you will learn about the different ways of working that are known as flexible working.

Finally you will learn about the growing importance of environmentally friendly work practices. You will understand the different ways that waste can be reduced in the workplace. For example, the use of resources such as paper, printer cartridges and electricity is kept as low as possible in many workplaces, and well-known businesses such as Marks & Spencer have detailed long-term plans for reducing the use of resources, such as unnecessary packaging and carrier bags.

3.1 The working environment

The open-plan office

The **open-plan office** means that most employees work in the same space. Their desks might be arranged so that people in the same team or department are near to each other. Partitions or screens can be used to make separate work spaces. This is the way most offices are organised.

A An open-plan office

Advantages of the open-plan office

- Employees can work together as a team as it is easy to communicate with the people they work with.
- People feel less isolated and more aware of what is happening in their workplace.
- Faxes, printers, photocopiers and other equipment can easily be shared.
- Managers are more accessible.
- It is easier to supervise other people as they can be seen and they can easily ask for help from their manager.

Disadvantages of the open-plan office

- It can be noisy and this might distract employees from their work.
- There is a lack of privacy which makes confidential conversations more difficult.
- Some employees might feel that they are being 'watched' by their managers.
- It might be easier to lose or mislay documents in a busy environment shared with others.

The cellular office

Using lots of very small office spaces is a more traditional way of working. The workplace would have lots of small offices where, often, one person works alone. They will be able to close their door and work privately. In a **cellular office** the environment would look and feel very different from the open-plan system.

Objectives

Understand the features of different types of office layout.

Understand the advantages and disadvantages of office layouts.

Be able to decide when a layout is suitable for a particular situation.

Key terms

Open-plan office: an office layout which is one room with few or no partitions, where everyone works in a shared space.

Cellular office: a workplace that has many small office spaces where doors can be closed and small numbers of people work in them.

Case study

In 2007, Penguin Books refurbished its offices on The Strand, in central London, and made it completely open plan. Everyone from the Chief Executive Officer to the student on work experience has a desk for all to see.

When Penguin first suggested a move to open plan, there was an extreme reaction. Directors and editors flapped, gossiped and even drummed up a petition in protest.

See www.thebookseller.com/in-depth/feature/48378-open-plan-office-politics.html for more detail.

What do you think about the reaction of directors to this change? Do you think Penguin Books was right to change its offices?

Advantages of the cellular office

- The work environment is quiet and private.
- Meetings can be held privately, which may make the people involved feel more comfortable.
- For some people 'higher up' the business structure, their own office is seen as a sign of their seniority.
- Security is better as documents and files are less likely to be moved by others and the office might be lockable.

Disadvantages of the cellular office

- It is harder for a manager to supervise the work of others as they are not physically in the same space.
- More equipment might need to be bought, such as printers and photocopiers, as sharing is less practical.
- Some people might feel isolated and not in touch with what is going on in the rest of the workplace.
- Social time is restricted to break and lunchtimes.

What will happen in practice?

Most offices will use a combination of open-plan and cellular workspace. How it is organised will depend on the following issues.

The business and its work

Team working

In many businesses people work together in teams. The members of a sales team for a brand of chocolate might look after sales to different parts of the country, but they will need to know about others' work. The open-plan office is better suited to team working.

Creativity

A business developing a new brand of shampoo will need the people working on this task to have an appropriate workspace. As well as computers, they might use drawing boards, flip charts and need space to look at existing makes of shampoo which they are competing against. Their space might be cellular because they have their own room, but open-plan within that room to allow a group to work on a variety of tasks.

Efficiency and quality

Sometimes the office will be planned so that as many people as possible can work in a space and that they work **efficiently**. Call centres are an example of this. Many call centre operators can be fitted into a typical office. With a telephone and computer, they can deal with a large volume of work.

The quality of call centre operators is monitored closely. The open-plan office makes supervision of workers easier and this can lead to people doing their job better than if they were more isolated.

AQA *Examiner's tip*

You will need to make a recommendation about which sort of workplace organisation is the best for a particular task. You will need to justify your choice.

Did you know ??????

Office Angels, the recruitment business, did a survey of 1,500 workers and found that 84 per cent preferred closed rather than open-plan offices. They also said that they would like offices to have the following: big-screen TVs, tropical fish, cappuccino makers, games consoles, neck massage and natural air and light. See www.flexibility.co.uk.

Activity

1 Investigate an office that you are familiar with. It could be from work experience, a class visit or an office in your school.

a Draw the layout.

b Describe whether it is open-plan, cellular or a mixture of both.

c Explain how the office organisation helps the work to be done efficiently.

d Are there any features from the Office Angels survey in this office?

e How well do you think the workplace layout helps the business to carry out its work?

Key terms

Efficient: when time, space or energy is used with as little waste as possible.

3.2 Effective workplace design

You have considered the general layout of a workplace in section 3.1. We are now going to look in more detail about how the design of the workplace affects workers' wellbeing and how they work.

■ Ergonomics

Ergonomics means studying people and their working environment to make the two things 'fit' with each other. This will involve looking at any equipment, furniture or machinery which they may use and making sure that it is designed so that the person can do their job as effectively as possible. **Ergonomics** covers a wide variety of equipment used, but here you will think about a typical office environment.

What the ergonomist will do

The ergonomist will look at the job being done and the person doing it. The two should 'fit' so that the job does not cause injury to the person.

The office environment

You will consider the typical furniture and equipment found in an office and how they should 'fit' the user.

Seats

Seats should be adjustable so that users of different sizes can use them. A good office seat should have the following features:

- adjustable height so that the user's legs are neither dangling in the air nor squashed up against their desk
- the height of the back rest should be adjustable and it should tilt for more comfort
- a seat pan (the part you sit on) that tilts
- arm rests that can be removed if they are not wanted (they can stop the user getting near enough to their desk)
- a five-castor base for good stability.

The person using the seat should understand how to adjust it for maximum comfort and good posture.

Desks

A good office desk should have the following:

- enough space for paperwork, a computer including the monitor, a keyboard and mouse, and for anything else used
- enough leg space, so drawers and supports should not get in the way of the employee's legs
- an adjustable height is not a feature of many desks, but they are good for very tall or short people.

A *A good office environment includes a comfortable, adjustable chair and a desk with plenty of space on and around it*

Computers

The main parts of a computer that cause problems for users are the keyboard, the mouse and the monitor. There are now various supports that can be bought to support the wrist. The monitor display should be clear and easy to read, adjustable for colour, contrast, brightness, tilt and swivel, and have no flicker.

The ideal workstation

The **workstation** is the combination of furniture and equipment used by an employee. Diagram **B** shows the correct posture someone should have when working in an office environment.

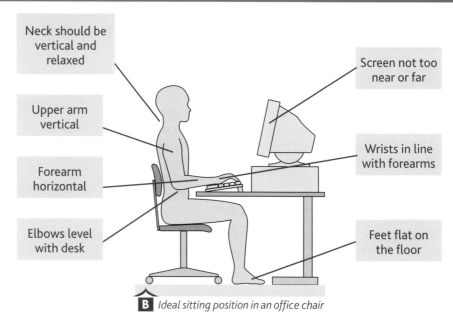

Neck should be vertical and relaxed

Screen not too near or far

Upper arm vertical

Wrists in line with forearms

Forearm horizontal

Elbows level with desk

Feet flat on the floor

B   *Ideal sitting position in an office chair*

■ The consequences of poor workplace design

Creating an effective workplace means spending time talking to workers to make sure that they are comfortable and know how to adjust their environment if necessary. It also means spending money on buying specialist equipment. If these things are not done, there are several possible consequences:

- employees taking time off work because of injuries or back pain
- less work done as people are uncomfortable and, therefore, less effective
- cases of repetitive strain injury (RSI) as a result of keyboard use (this and other issues are considered on pages 30–31).

Activity

1   You have been asked to order office furniture for a client who needs:

- ten chairs and desks suitable for computer use
- two chairs suitable for the reception area
- a coffee table for the reception area.

The client would like you to explore two choices for each item needed and for you to make a final recommendation.

a   Produce your findings as a word-processed report incorporating pictures of the items you recommend and their total cost.

b   Justify your recommendation.

There are a large number of websites that sell office furniture which will provide this information. You could also collect brochures from shops such as Staples. See **www.staples.co.uk** for information and local stores.

▉ Employers' responsibilities

Employers must provide a safe working environment for their employees. There are laws that cover the things the employer must do. The places where most accidents happen are building sites, however this section concentrates on places of work where ICT equipment is used – there are plenty of hazards even in an office.

The Health and Safety at Work Act

The main point from this legislation is that the employer must make sure that the workplace is safe. The Act requires things such as:

- safe entry and exit into and out of buildings
- enough toilets and facilities for getting drinks
- proper maintenance of equipment
- employee training about health and safety issues that relate to their job
- the display of information about health and safety matters.

Display screen regulations

These **regulations** have been passed because many people now spend much of their working lives in front of a computer screen. The **display screen regulations** are generally sensible guidelines for computer users and much of it links to workplace organisation which we studied on pages 28–29.

Main points of the regulations

- The computer screen should be a reasonable size and the brightness and contrast should be adjustable.
- Keyboards should be separate from the screen and the user should be able to tilt it.
- There should not be any glare from the sun or lights onto the screen.
- Desks, chairs and footrests should all be the right sort for office use.
- The user must be allowed to take breaks from using the screen.
- Software used should be 'user friendly'.

A *The display screen regulations were passed to protect workers who spend a lot of time using computer screens*

Objectives

Understand why it is important that employers provide a safe working environment.

Understand how health and safety regulations affect users of ICT.

Did you know ??????

In 2006–2007, 30 million work days were lost due to work-related ill-health and 6 million due to workplace injury. 2.2 million people suffered from an illness they believed was caused, or made worse, by work.

Source: www.hse.gov.uk

Key terms

Regulation: an official rule or law.

Display screen regulations: the official rules to protect people whose work involves using a computer screen.

⦿⦿ links

For more detailed information on the regulations go to **www.opsi.gov.uk**.

AQA Examiner's tip

You might need to advise a business on what changes must be made to meet health and safety requirements.

Consequences of neglecting employees' health and safety

At worst a fatal accident could happen at work. Most workplace accidents and injuries are not fatal but can cause misery for the worker and cost and inconvenience for the employer. In an office environment typical hazards are:

- cables, which someone could trip over
- cabinets and cupboards that might obstruct doorways and fire exits
- electrical faults with equipment
- RSI (repetitive strain injury) and other aches and pains from sitting at a computer for too long
- eye strain and headaches.

If these things happen, the employer could be affected in several ways:

- employees take time off work because they are injured or ill
- someone else might be needed to fill their job, which will be costly
- if the injury is serious, compensation might have to be paid
- the business could end up with a bad reputation as an unsafe place to work.

Employees' responsibilities

The employee should also take responsibility for their health and safety at work. This means that they must behave in a way that does not affect the health and safety of others. Things such as drinking alcohol or taking illegal drugs could create a danger to other workers. Before the ban on smoking in public places, an employee could have considered suing their employer if they were affected by the smoke from work colleagues. It seems hard to believe that it was not so long ago that people were freely smoking at their desks at work.

C *Workers can get RSI from typing on a keyboard for too long*

No smoking beyond this point

B *The smoking ban protects employees' health*

Activity

Design a leaflet using suitable software that could be given to all members of staff informing them about health and safety issues related to working in an office.

The aim of the leaflet is to show, in an interesting way, the main features of health and safety regulations and the display screen regulations. The leaflet should have plenty of pictures and graphics, so that workers can see easily how the regulations apply to them.

New working practices

The traditional way of working, where someone goes to the same place to work for a set number of hours, is changing. You have just considered the physical equipment that someone needs to be comfortable and free from aches and pains. However, some people do not have any permanent workspace which is their own.

Hot desking

Hot desking is when employees are not given a desk or workstation of their own. Instead, they share desks and equipment as they need it. This works if the employee does not spend a great deal of time in the office. It would be wasteful to give an employee a permanent desk if it is often left unused. Laptop computers, wireless networks and mobile phones all make this way of working much easier.

Hot desking works when:

- the work being done is carried out in different places
- the employee has the right technology (e.g. a mobile phone so that he or she can always be contacted)
- there are enough 'hot desks' so that one is available when the employee needs it
- all the shared equipment is maintained properly.

Hot desking doesn't work when:

- employees need to be 'found' easily
- there are not enough 'hot desks', so an employee cannot do his or her work
- different technology and equipment is needed, not all of which is portable.

Whether hot desking suits a particular business will depend on the work being done and the way the company wants to treat employees. Hot desking can create an environment where there are no workspaces that feel 'owned' by anyone and less team working and social time may be possible. On the other hand, some businesses create very pleasant spaces for hot desking and socialising which works well.

Teleconferencing and video conferencing

New technology means people can communicate even when they are not physically in the same room. Of course, the telephone has been around a long time and the mobile phone is an everyday item. These are excellent for two people to have a conversation, but advances in technology mean that there are now ways to speak to more than one person.

Teleconferencing

Teleconferencing is a system of having a telephone conversation with more than one person. It is also sometimes called a 'conference call'. BT has a conference call system called 'Conference Call Meet Me' which allows up to 20 people to talk to each other at the same time. You might like to consider the practicalities of that!

Objectives

Understand how new technologies are changing how and where employees do their jobs.

Recommend the use of new technology where it is appropriate.

Key terms

Hot desking: workers do not have their own desk but share workspace as it is needed.

Teleconferencing: technology that allows more than one person to participate in a telephone conversation/ meeting. Participants might not be in the same building or even in the same country.

Video conferencing

Video conferencing is an extension of the conference call in that participants can see as well as hear several people who are not actually in the same room as them. Technically there are various ways in which this can be done to suit the numbers of people and the location. BT has many systems that do this, and which aim to offer 'real-time' communication so that the meeting is not affected by time lags. Webcams are used to link people visually. See **www.conferencing. bt.com** for more information on this technology.

Key terms

Video conferencing: similar to teleconferencing, but where the participants are able to see one another and share computer files.

A *Video conferencing*

AQA *Examiner's tip*

You might be asked when these technologies could be a good way of communicating.

Benefits of these technologies

- Money is saved because people do not have to travel to meetings; particularly good if it is an international meeting.
- Teleconferencing provides a quick, inexpensive way of communicating with colleagues who are not often in the office.

Drawbacks of these technologies

- Teleconferencing can be difficult with large numbers; the call must be managed so that everyone can have a chance to participate.
- An important part of communication is eye contact and reading facial expression; this cannot be done with teleconferencing.
- Video conferencing requires expensive equipment in the offices of all the participants in the conference.
- Some would say that it is never the same as being in the same room as those you want to communicate with. (Chapter 7 looks at communication in more detail.)

Activity

Using a suitable software program, design a leaflet aimed at a business, explaining when hot desking, teleconferencing and video conferencing are suitable and unsuitable ways of communicating. Use examples and pictures to illustrate the content.

Search the BBC's business pages for stories on these business technologies at **news.bbc.co.uk**.

What is flexible working?

A recurring theme in this book is change. It is a fact of working life. Jobs do not just mean working in one place from 9 till 5 every day. Flexible working means the way people are actually employed is changing. More people are now wanting or needing to work more flexible hours to fit in with their lifestyle, or want to work from home.

Home and teleworking

Some people have always worked from home. An author usually works from home, though some hire office space so that they feel they are 'going to work'. Computers, telephones and broadband connections mean that **teleworking** is possible for more people. What is changing is the increasing number of people who want to do at least some of their work at home, when in the past they would have gone to an office to do it.

Advantages of homeworking:

- no time is wasted travelling (or commuting) to work
- it is more environmentally friendly as no travelling is involved
- there are fewer distractions at home, compared to a busy office
- it can fit around other commitments, such as childcare
- there is no need to dress for work.

Disadvantages of homeworking:

- some people might not like the isolation and prefer a busy office; no social opportunities
- there can be distractions at home
- it can be hard to 'go to work' in the same place that you live the rest of your life; do you set 'work hours'?
- it is easy to lose touch with your work colleagues.

Others forms of flexible working

Other ways of organising how work is done can be viewed as flexible.

Flexi-time

Flexi-time is when an employee has a core work time (perhaps 10am to 4pm) and they can organise the rest of their hours as they wish, as long as enough hours are worked in total. In some jobs, if more hours are worked over a month, they can be used as free time in the next month.

Objectives

Understand a range of flexible work practices.

Understand the impact they have on a business and the working lives of employees.

Key terms

Teleworking: using broadband connections, computers and mobile phones to work from home for some or all of the week.

Flexi-time: an arrangement where the working day has core hours that must be worked and then flexibility to work the remaining hours as the employee chooses.

Day	Start in	Finish out	Hours worked	Breaks	Total (minus breaks)
Monday	8.00	16.30	8.30	1.00	7.30
Tuesday	8.30	17.00	8.30	1.00	7.30
Wednesday	8.00	17.30	9.30	2.00	7.30
Thursday	8.30	16.30	8.00	0.30	7.30
Friday	9.00	17.00	8.00	1.00	7.00
					Total 37

Name:..

Department: Acquistions   Contracted hours: 37   For week ending: 03-Apr-09

I certify that the hours above were worked:

Signed: ....Date: ....

A *A flexi-time timesheet*

Job sharing

This means that two people split the work of a full-time job between them. This works very well for some work, for example, primary school teaching jobs can work well as a job share. In 2004 a husband and wife team were appointed to job share the head teacher post at a primary school in Nottingham. Many public sector jobs are open to applications from job sharers.

Seasonal and shift work

Some businesses will offer workers flexible working patterns because they are not needed permanently. Alton Towers theme park employs much of its workforce seasonally to fit in with its busy times of year. As shops increase their opening hours, workers will work in shifts to cover them.

Flexible working from the employee's point of view

Employees who are able to benefit from flexible work practices usually feel much more positive about their work. They can have a better balance between work and home life. Often it means that they can keep a job which, without a flexible approach from their employer, they would have had to leave. The web-based organisation **www.workingfamilies.org** highlights many case studies of employers such as Dyson, The Body Shop and Jaguar, who have offered flexible working. For women, in particular, it can mean that looking after a family does not mean completely giving up their career.

> **AQA   Examiner's tip**
>
> Not all these flexible work practices will be appropriate for every type of job. Think about which sort of work can more easily be arranged flexibly or shared.

B *Flexible work practices, such as working from home, can have many positive aspects*

Activity

1   Carry out this activity in groups.

a   Research which employers offer flexible working. Use websites such as **www.bbc.co.uk/business** and **www.workingfamilies.org.uk** and job advertisements on websites and in newspapers. Local authorities often offer flexible working – you could investigate what your local authority offers.

b   Research how many people you know have flexible working arrangements and the nature of their work.

c   Report back your findings using a suitable method of communication.

3.6 Using resources with consideration

The importance of using resources with consideration

We all use up resources as we carry out our daily activities. Unless you walk or cycle everywhere, the journeys you make use up fuel. The business world also is a huge consumer of resources and energy.

In the 21st century, there is a growing awareness that we cannot continue to use up resources without considering how we can replace them. There will come a point when there is no more coal or oil to use as fuel. We need to find sources of energy and raw materials which are **sustainable**.

New ways of approaching business

There are many words and phrases in use that describe how businesses want to operate. They tell us they want to be '**environmentally friendly**', reduce their 'carbon footprint' or be 'carbon neutral'. These terms mean that they want to work without using more resources than are necessary. Carbon neutral means that the carbon a business puts into the air from using cars or machinery in factories is balanced out by doing something that removes carbon from the air, such as planting trees. More businesses are now aiming to make their business practices sustainable.

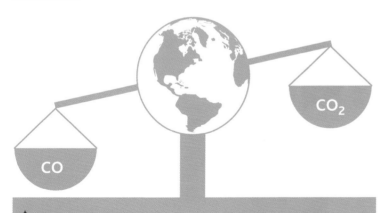

A *Some companies try to balance their carbon emissions by investing in carbon-reduction products*

Source: www.carbonmanagers.com

What are the main resources businesses use?

In a typical office the main resources that are used are electricity, paper and printer ink. In shops such as supermarkets waste comes from foods that cannot be sold because they have passed their 'sell by' date and from the packaging in which food arrives and is sold.

For supermarkets, 'food miles' are a big challenge. Supermarkets are now trying to source fresh foods locally and more seasonally. For example, it is likely that the British strawberries in your local supermarket will come from a local grower.

Objectives

Understand the growing importance of 'environmentally friendly' practices.

Understand practical ways that businesses can use resources in a more environmentally friendly way.

Key terms

Sustainable: business activities that can continue over a period of time without harming the environment.

Environmentally friendly: carrying out activities in such a way that they do not harm the environment.

Did you know ??????

According to research from the Carbon Trust, an average office-based business wastes £6,000 per year by leaving equipment on at weekends and bank holidays.

Source: www.hie.co.uk

Case study

Marks & Spencer's Plan A

Marks & Spencer's Plan A is an ambitious environmental project which has several aims.

There are many projects taking place under this plan, which range from no longer giving free bags with food purchases, to a clothes recycling agreement with Oxfam.

Go to their website **www.plana.marksandspencer.com** to find out more. Do you think that Marks & Spencer can achieve these aims?

How resources can be saved

Paper

- Consider whether everything needs to be printed; some documents can be transferred electronically by e-mail.
- Use a printer that prints on two sides of the paper.
- Use paper that has been made from recycled sources.

Printer ink and cartridges

- Consider whether something needs to be printed in the first place.
- Use cartridges that can be refilled.
- **Recycle** old cartridges.
- Some charities will collect and recycle cartridges.

Electricity

- Turn off all equipment overnight.
- Turn off computers not in use, instead of leaving them in standby mode.
- Use a thermostat to control heating and turn it off completely overnight.
- Replace air conditioning with natural ventilation.
- Use low-energy light bulbs and make more use of natural light.

Fuel

- If goods are delivered in vans or lorries, low-energy vehicles could be considered.
- Company cars must not have large engines that consume a lot of petrol.
- Encourage employees to travel to work by public transport, bicycle or walking.
- Encourage car sharing.

Problems with environmentally friendly practices

Some employees will need to be convinced that it is important that the practices the business decides on are carried out. Some workers might not want to change their work practices.

- Some changes, such as investing in low-energy vehicles or low-energy equipment, mean spending quite a lot of money.
- It can take a little more effort to carry out some of these guidelines; some people might prefer to work as they used to do.
- Removing air conditioning or reducing heat could create resentment among some employees.
- Some employees might feel that it is not up to their employer to suggest that they do not drive to work.

B *Recycling is an important feature of an environmentally friendly workplace*

∞**links**

The following websites might be useful for the activity:
www.netregs.gov.uk
www.businessdata.co.uk
www.businesslink.gov.uk

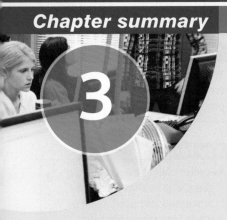

3

In this chapter you have learnt:

✔ about the two main types of office layout and when they are suitable

✔ why it is important that people use work stations that are designed to meet their needs, so that injuries are avoided

✔ how health and safety legislation makes sure that people are safe at work when using ICT equipment

✔ when new technologies and working practices are appropriate and be able to recommend situations when they could be used

✔ how working in an environmentally friendly way is becoming more important to businesses and how they can do this.

Revision questions

1 Write a clear definition of the following terms:

a ergonomics

b flexi-time

c hot desking

d open-plan office

e cellular office

f environmentally-friendly.

2 Jay Shah runs a travel agency that sells holidays to the public. The agency is organised so that the six employees each have a suitable seat and desk with computer and a monitor. There are two chairs on the other side of their desk for customers to sit on. The agency is open-plan, but Jay has tried to put as much space as possible between each workstation so that customers' conversations have some privacy.

One of the agency staff, Paul, has asked Jay if he can work more flexibly, as he wants to be able to take his children to school on three mornings a week.

a Describe two ways in which the chairs that the employees sit on will be different to the chairs that are used for the customers.

b Explain why an open-plan layout is more suitable for this sort of business than putting each employee in a cellular office.

c Jay has suggested to Paul that he could work flexi-time. Explain what this means and whether you think it would be suitable for this sort of job.

4 Security of data

In this chapter

4.1 ICT data systems in business

4.2 Methods of protecting data

4.3 Data protection and the law

This chapter is about handling data and you will learn how businesses must take great care of the data they deal with.

You will learn that data comes from primary and secondary sources and that data can be gathered electronically or manually. Data has to be put into a system and you will learn about the different methods of doing this.

You will continue with this theme by finding out about the different ways that data can be stored and retrieved for use. You will learn which methods are most appropriate. For example, sometimes a printout of a document is the most useful way of handling the data, whereas on other occasions a presentation using a projector might be more appropriate.

You will then consider why keeping data secure is so important. You will look at examples of when important data has been lost or stolen. You will be able to recommend appropriate ways in which a business could keep the data it handles secure.

Learning about data protection is relevant to the whole of this chapter as it considers the legal requirements that businesses must follow when storing data. You will learn how this affects what a business can do with the data it holds and the rights people have over the data stored about them.

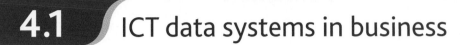

4.1 ICT data systems in business

Data sources

Businesses deal with data from a wide variety of places. A shop will need to collect and store data on the goods it sells, while even the smallest business will need to keep data about its employees. **Primary data** could come from market research collected from customers about their views on a product. **Secondary data** is also used by businesses. For example, in 2008 the chef Jamie Oliver opened three Italian-style restaurants. He will have researched the places he has chosen (Oxford, Bath and Kingston) by looking at secondary data. This will inform him about things such as the average income of people in these towns or how many other restaurants are already there.

Chapter 2 discussed the importance of good systems for processing, storing and retrieving this data. We are now going to look at how data can be captured and put into an ICT system.

Manual data-capture methods

Data capture means the way that data is collected, recorded and then entered into a computer using a suitable **input device**.

Paper-based questionnaires

Example

You want to set up a restaurant to rival Jamie Oliver's in your own town. Before you open, you will want to know something about what people like to eat in restaurants and how much they are willing to spend. This will give you some primary data which you can then put into a computer system and process so that it is useful to you.

You need to create a data-capture form to do this. This will be a paper-based form that will make it as easy as possible to gather the responses from the people and make it easy to input the findings into your computer.

Your simple data-capture form will record the age range and gender of the people you ask, as well as food preferences and the maximum amount they are willing to spend on a meal in a restaurant. The number of rows will match the number of people you ask.

Person	Male (M) or Female (F)?	Range					Food style		Max. spend (£)
		16–30	31–40	41–50	51–60	61+	Italian	English	
1									
2									
3									
4									
5									

A A typical data capture form

Forms that can be read by optical mark recognition (OMR)

You might have filled in a form or done a multiple-choice test at school where you had to fill in boxes using a pencil. These sheets are designed to be put into a computer system by using a scanner and software that recognises the marks made on the paper. Teachers submit coursework marks to examination boards in this way, though electronic systems are being introduced.

Electronic data-capture systems

Businesses can collect data electronically. A teacher might now be asked to input their coursework marks straight into a system used by the examination board. When you buy a bag of crisps from a supermarket, scanning the bar code on the crisp packet will send the data from that bar code to the store's computer system. When goods are paid for by a credit or debit card, the details of the account from which the money will be taken are held on the magnetic strip on the back of the card.

Choosing the most appropriate method

The method of data capture used needs to give the most accurate information possible. Our survey of people's preferences of restaurant food will be cheap to organise as it is paper-based. The problem is that mistakes could easily be made by the person manually filling in the data-capture form. An electronic system is much more expensive to set up because specialist equipment is needed, but there is less chance of mistakes being made.

B *Data on this form is read electronically*

■ Data input devices

Data input devices are computer hardware supported by software called drivers. They are the way that a user inputs data into the computer.

C *A computer keyboard*

D *A computer mouse*

Activity

1 Design a data-capture form to find out about people's leisure activities in your class. Your design should make the findings easy to input into a computer system.

Different data input devices

E

Input devices	Description
Keyboard	The data from your restaurant survey can be entered into a database or spreadsheet using a keyboard.
Mouse	This is a pointing device which is used to move the cursor across a computer screen. Most computer users will use a mouse and a keyboard as their main input devices.
Scanner	Reads images or text and converts the data to digital signals. Most scanners can read both text and graphics. For example, a picture may be scanned and then the size or colour may be changed. A scanner can be part of a machine which is also a printer and a photocopier.
Digital camera	A digital camera records an image either onto built-in memory or onto a removable memory card. Once a picture has been taken it can be downloaded to a computer system. Photos can be edited, incorporated into documents, sent by e-mail or posted onto websites.
Webcam	This is usually mounted on top of a computer monitor. A webcam can transmit live action and a microphone can be used to add sound. In business the webcam can do the same job as video conferencing camera if just two people need to see and speak to each other.
Voice recognition system	This is software which can recognise the spoken word when a microphone is used as an input device. This software is not perfect as it will not always recognise every word spoken and will put incorrect ones in. It can be very useful if large quantities of text need to be put into a system.

Storage devices

The huge amount of data a business handles needs to be stored securely and accessed easily. There are several **storage devices** that can be used.

Different types of storage devices

F

Input devices	Description
Hard disk	This is the main storage device used and is part of the computer. Computer hard disks can usually store more data than laptop hard disks. The hard disk has the capacity to store enough data for most needs, though graphics files take up more space than text-only files. A backup copy of stored data should be kept, and this should be on a separate drive to the original copy so that data can be retrieved if the hard disk fails.
Compact Discs (CD)	There are several sorts of disks. The benefits of them are that they can store a lot of data: **CD-ROM**: These are 'read only' which means that the data held on them can't be changed. Think of a music CD which you buy – you cannot change the music or add to it. New computer software comes on a set of CD-ROMs **CD-R**: These discs allow new data to be put on a blank disc, but they are 'write once', 'read only'. So once the data is on the disc it cannot be edited. This may be beneficial if it is very important that the data is not altered in anyway. This is sometimes referred to as being 'burning on' to the disc because lasers are used to do just that. **CD-RW**: The 'RW' means rewrite. These discs can be wiped and reused. They are more expensive that CD-Rs, though the type of disc a business chooses to use will depend on the nature of the information being stored.
Digital Versatile Disc (DVDs)	Like CDs but hold more data. The video playback is much better quality but the blank discs are much more expensive than CDs. There are various sorts of DVDs, which can hold different amounts of data and some are recordable and re-writable. Blu-ray offers storage up to five times that of a conventional DVD.
USB (Universal Serial Bus) Memory Stick	Memory sticks are great for storing data and for taking it from one place to another. Today 16 GB sticks are available which are large enough to store most files. They can be plugged straight into a USB port on a computer and used as an additional drive. The size does make them easy to lose, which at best is really annoying but at worst can mean very important data getting into the wrong hands.

Key terms

Storage device: a piece of equipment capable of storing electronic data.

Output device: equipment that can show the data stored in a computer.

G A hard disk

H CDs and DVDs look the same but DVDs hold more data

I A USB memory stick

Output devices

Computer users need to get the information in their computer out of it in some way. To do this an **output device** is required. The most obvious way is either to view data on the screen or monitor or to print it out.

Monitors

Monitors come in various sizes and specifications depending on what they are to be used for. The monitor is useful if data simply needs to be viewed as it is being inputted or processed. It is less useful if large numbers of people need to view the data or if a paper copy is needed. See **www.webopedia.com** for more technical detail on various types of monitors.

Projectors

Projectors are extremely useful when larger numbers of people need to see some information. It is very likely that each classroom in your school or college has a computer with a projector attached to it. In businesses, it means that presentations can be shown to large numbers of people. The price of projector units has fallen but the replacement bulbs are very expensive.

Printers

Printers are output devices that produce a hard (or paper) copy of information stored in a computer. Laser printers very quickly produce high-quality text and graphics that do not smear. Laser printers used to be expensive but continue to come down in price. Toner cartridges last longer than cartridges for inkjet printers, for the same volume of printing. Laser printers that can print in colour are more expensive than those that just print in black and white.

Inkjet printers tend to be cheaper and smaller than laser printers. They can print in black and white and colour. The quality is not quite as good as laser quality but fine for relatively small numbers of copies.

Choose a laser printer if …

- you have a relatively high budget to spend
- you want to print a lot of high-quality copies
- the speed of printing is important
- you want to keep running costs down.

Choose an inkjet printer if …

- you do not want to spend too much on buying a printer
- you do not have a large volume of printing
- you do not mind a slower print speed
- you want to be able to print in colour on different sorts of paper.

Did you know ??????

In 2007 the government lost computer discs which held the personal and bank details of 25 million people who receive child benefits. To date, they have not been found!

AQA Examiner's tip

The examiner will expect you to know when a piece of equipment is suitable for a certain work situation. Justifying a recommendation you make is an important skill for this examination.

Think about it

Why do you think that projectors and laser printers are continuing to become cheaper to buy, but toner cartridges and replacement bulbs are very expensive?

Find out some prices for projector bulbs and toner cartridges.

See **www.inkshop.co.uk/ comparing_inkjet_and_ laser_printers.php** for more information.

Activity

2   Penny needs advice. She is setting up a business as an odd-job person. She is going to produce a leaflet explaining the sorts of jobs she will do such as cleaning, gardening, assembling flat-pack furniture or even taking and collecting things from the dry cleaners. She will be based at home and will need some ICT equipment. You have a budget of £1,000 to spend. She needs the following:

- A computer or laptop with suitable software for producing letters, leaflets and keeping records of customer details and her accounts.
- A printer for printing the leaflets advertising her services.

- A digital camera so that she can use photos to illustrate her leaflet.

She wants to produce 500 copies of her leaflet. What do you recommend she does?

- Produce a word-processed report, including pictures of the items you recommend, explaining why you have chosen this equipment. For each item, explain why it is the best choice for her.

- There is a huge number of websites selling ICT equipment where you can find out what is available.

4.2 Methods of protecting data

Businesses deal with all sorts of data which is stored electronically. There are lots of benefits of storing data in this way but it also creates many possible ways of losing it or of it being stolen. The sort of data that might be at risk of being stolen or used by someone outside or external to the business could be:

- information such as sales figures
- customers' names and addresses – possibly extremely useful to a competitor because they could potentially 'steal' your customers.

Inside the business, data should also be made secure as not all internal users should have access to all the stored data. Personal details about employees should not be accessible to everyone, only those who need it to do their job.

Keeping the hardware safe

The obvious starting point is to make sure that the rooms your computers are in are secure. This means simple measures such as locking doors and windows when the rooms are not in use. Laptops and computers should also have their serial numbers recorded so that if they are stolen there is more chance of getting them back. There might need to be rules about who can take laptops home and how they will be stored. Specialist locks, such as the Kensington Lock, are designed to secure hardware to desks. Backups should also be kept secure and in a different location to the original data.

A *Laptop security lock cable*

Keeping data safe from external access

Although computer networks are usually safe from outsiders accessing files on them, some computer 'hackers' will find a way into a network if they are determined enough. A former computer hacker, Cal Leeming, was able to steal details and money from thousands of credit cards. He now advises businesses on how to make their systems secure.

Ways of securing data from external access

People on the outside of a business might want to get into a computer system either to steal data or to cause disruption. Computer **viruses**

Objectives

Understand the importance of data security.

Understand the ways that data can be made secure and when they are appropriate.

Did you know ??????

In 2007 a laptop was stolen from someone's house which contained personal data about 26,000 people who were in the Marks & Spencer company pension scheme.

Source: www.theregister.co.uk

Did you know ??????

Two password-protected CDs containing data about all the recipients of child benefits were sent unrecorded and unregistered by a junior HMRC official through courier TNT to the National Audit Office on 18 October 2007, but never arrived and have not been found.

Source: www.silicon.com/research

Key terms

Virus: a program or code that runs on your computer against your wishes. It can replicate itself and can soon take up all the available memory and bring the system to a standstill. Virus protection software should be used to detect a virus before it causes damage.

are often sent via email attachments and their sole purpose is to cause huge inconvenience. Ways of securing a system from external access include:

- installing virus protection software which will routinely scan all incoming emails and check them for viruses
- training staff to beware of emails with attachments from unknown senders
- using a **firewall**
- using **encryption**
- Making sure that a **wireless network** is password-protected to prevent **unauthorised access**
- having strict rules about who takes home laptops, disks and memory sticks
- having strict rules about what can be posted, such as disks and memory sticks.

■ Securing data inside a business

Inside a business it is likely that not everyone should be able to access all of the data on the computer system. Some people will have **authorised access** to data to which other people will not. A headteacher in a school will probably have access to more data than other staff. This could be because some data contains private details of individual members of staff.

Ways of restricting access to authorised users inside a business

Methods include:

- the use of user names and **passwords** that allow people to access only the data they need for work reasons
- changing passwords regularly and encouraging people to keep them secret
- making some files 'read only' so that important data cannot be changed.

Activities

1 For each of these situations, explain what should be done to protect the data or computer:

a   A business taking people's credit card details on a website.

b   A school wanting students to access only certain parts of its network.

c   A home computer user is worried about viruses getting onto their computer.

d   An employee wants to take a laptop home to do some work over the weekend.

e   A file must be accessed by all employees but the data must not be changed.

2 Use websites to research how many cases of lost data and identity theft have been in the news recently. Report back your findings to your class. Discuss how this relates to what you have learned from this chapter.

Data protection and the law

■ The Data Protection Act

The Data Protection Act (1998) exists to make sure that any personal (e.g. names, addresses, bank details) or sensitive data (e.g. religious beliefs, criminal records) on paper files or computer is stored and used appropriately. For example, a hospital must keep patient data secure as it is personal and must not be made public. Any business or organisation that holds personal data must register with the **Information Commissioner**, so that it is known that they hold personal data.

Main principles of the Data Protection Act

1 The data must be collected fairly and lawfully.

2 Data must only be held for the reasons given to the Information Commissioner, such as holding customers' addresses for delivering goods.

3 You can only use the data for the reasons you said you would, when you registered. For example, you cannot give it away or sell it unless you said you would.

4 You should only hold as much data as you need to do the job you said you were doing. So the data held about Tesco Clubcard holders does not need to include their national insurance number.

5 The data must be accurate and kept up to date. A student's record of test and examination results should be up to date so that the latest information is used as a reference.

6 Data should not be held if it is no longer needed. The details of people who are no longer customers should not be kept in a database.

7 Data held must be kept securely and not open to unauthorised access. In your school or college, your friends cannot access personal data about you.

8 Data can only be passed to other countries inside the European Economic Area (that's the EU plus some small European countries), unless that other country has a similar data protection law.

Objectives

Understand the main content of the Data Protection Act.

Understand how this constrains a business.

Key terms

Information Commissioner: the person who heads the Information Commissioner's Office, which aims to promote access to official information and protect personal data. See **www.ico.gov.uk** for more information.

Did you know ??????

Several banks have been criticised for dumping customers' personal data in bins outside their premises. Among them were HBOS, Alliance & Leicester, Royal Bank of Scotland, NatWest, Barclays Bank, Cooperative Bank and Nationwide Building Society.

Source: news.bbc.co.uk

Did you know ??????

In 2006–7, the Information Commissioner received nearly 24,000 enquiries or complaints about personal data issues.

Source: news.bbc.co.uk

A Banks have a duty to protect their customers' data

B The Data Protection Act

What rights people have under the Data Protection Act

As so much data is held about people (or data subjects as the Act calls them), people have rights over the data that is stored. These are:

- the right to see data held about them (they might have to pay to see it)
- the right to stop data that might cause damage or upset being processed – so a newspaper cannot publish how much a celebrity spends on champagne every month
- the right to have inaccurate or incorrect data changed – so if a patient record at a doctor's surgery has them down as a smoker, they can insist that the record is changed if they have given up
- the right to prevent data being used to send out junk mail, which might be electronic or paper.

AQA *Examiner's tip*

You will need to know the main principles of this Act and how it might affect different sorts of businesses.

Activity

The Data Protection Act applies to information used on social networking sites such as Facebook and Bebo. Using the Information Commission's website (**www.ico.gov.uk**) as a source of information, produce a leaflet for young people informing them how they can use social networking sites safely.

C Bebo

In this chapter you have learnt:

✔ about the different ways in which data can be gathered, put into, stored and retrieved from an ICT system

✔ about the importance of keeping this data secure and the ways that this can be done

✔ the main principles of the Data Protection Act (1998) and how it affects the way businesses handle the data they collect, store and disseminate.

Revision questions

1 Write a clear definition of each of the following methods of data protection and give an example of why they are used:

a a firewall

b encryption

c passwords.

2 State a situation when the following input device is the best way of putting data into an ICT system:

a mouse

b digital camera

c scanner.

3 Easy Bake is a business with three shops. Each shop bakes and sells various types of bread and cakes. Special occasion cakes can be ordered by customers.

Ben, the owner, is responsible for keeping all its computer records up to date. He has a database that holds data on the suppliers who provide Easy Bake with its ingredients, on the customer orders and on the staff he employs. He has no security on his computer system as he wants any of his staff to be able to use it.

a Give two examples of personal data that will be on this computer system.

b Describe two principles that the business must follow when holding data about its customers.

c Explain two rights that someone whose personal data is held on this computer system has in law.

d Explain two reasons why Ben should use some method of security on this computer.

e Describe one way that he could do this. Give reasons for your answer.

Ben wants to buy a better printer than the old one he uses. He wants to use it to print off price lists to display in the shops and documents showing the sorts of cakes that can be ordered. He might also print his own flyers to advertise the bakery.

f Describe the two main sorts of printer available and recommend which he should buy.

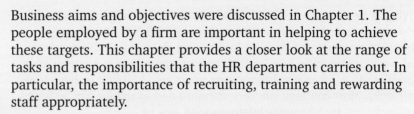

5 Recruitment and selection of staff

In this chapter

5.1 Contract of employment

5.2 How to recruit the right person for the job

5.3 Selecting the best candidate

5.4 Employment rights and responsibilities

Business aims and objectives were discussed in Chapter 1. The people employed by a firm are important in helping to achieve these targets. This chapter provides a closer look at the range of tasks and responsibilities that the HR department carries out. In particular, the importance of recruiting, training and rewarding staff appropriately.

The HR department carries out the following functions:

- recruitment selection and training of employees
- preparing contracts of employment
- overseeing negotiations about pay and working conditions
- supervising health and safety issues.

Throughout this chapter a case study will be used to illustrate the processes involved in the recruitment, selection and training of employees.

Case study

Riverdale Hotels Ltd

This is a privately owned business that runs 12 hotels across the UK and has its headquarters in Leicestershire. The company has a policy of promoting from within, so a lot of employees have worked for Riverdale for many years. However, it is always on the lookout for new recruits to join the team at any hotel in the group.

Riverdale Hotels Ltd employs people in the following areas:

Management: there is a Management Training Scheme for people who want to become assistant managers or hotel managers. The programme lasts 18 months and involves working at a number of hotels in the company. It is suitable for university graduates or people with good supervisory experience in hotels.

Front of house: this includes reception and portering services.

Restaurant: from waiters to the restaurant manager.

Housekeeping: this includes cleaning the public areas of the hotel and the bedrooms.

Catering: from the head chef to the kitchen porters, this includes all jobs linked to the preparation of food at the hotel.

The recruitment, selection and training of staff are very important in the hospitality industry because employees are the first point of contact with the customers and are the visual representation of the business.

When a new employee starts work, it is normal to receive a written document called a **contract of employment**. This is an agreement between an employer and employee about the terms and conditions of work. It should be kept and referred to when there is a potential problem (e.g. when employees want to arrange holidays or have time off sick). Most contracts are very standard and examples can be found on websites, such as **www.Business Link.gov.uk**.

Activity

1 In groups discuss whether or not it is important to have a written contract of employment rather than just a verbal agreement.

A contract of employment is a legal document and is very important because it protects both the employer and employee. It should contain the following features:

- job title/position – so the duties of the employee are clear
- place of work – the employer might expect the employee to work at more than one location
- hours of work – any extra hours may be considered overtime
- salary/wage rate – this should include the method and timing of payment.

These features are important because they can prevent misunderstanding and future disagreements, so new employees should always read through their contract carefully.

Types of contract of employment

Contracts of employment are not all the same, because people work under different basic conditions.

- **Full-time contracts** are for employees who normally work about 37.5 hours or 5 days per week.
- **Part-time contracts** are for employees who work a proportion of the full-time hours (e.g. 22.5 hours or 3 days per week).
- A **permanent contract** continues until the employee chooses to leave or retires.
- A **temporary contract,** or fixed-term contract, covers a specific period of time (e.g. one year or maternity leave).

Activity

2 Find out more about what should be in a contract of employment and your rights as an employee at **www.acas.org.uk**. Use all your knowledge to write a guide for students at your school or college.

Objectives

Understand the different types of contract of employment.

Know the most important features of a contract of employment.

Key terms

Contract of employment: agreement, usually written, about terms and conditions of employment.

Full-time contract: employment for standard hours.

Part-time contract: for a proportion of the full-time hours.

Permanent contract: continues indefinitely.

Temporary contract: applies for a stated period of time.

Did you know ??????

Many high-street shops and fast-food outlets expect employees to work at more than one location if required. This helps them cope with staff shortages due to sickness, for instance.

AQA Examiner's tip

Make sure that you understand why a contract of employment is important to an employer as well as an employee.

Riverdale Hotels Ltd

The new restaurant manager has been appointed at the White Hart Hotel, and she has been given a contract of employment by the company:

Name of Employer:	Riverdale Hotels Ltd
Name of Employee:	Lindsay Hamilton

Employment Start Date: 1st September 2008
Pay £18,000 per year paid monthly

Hours of work: 40 hours per week.
Any additional hours will be paid at rate of £12.00 per hour.

Holiday entitlement: 20 days per year to be taken out of season.

Notice of termination of employment: one month
Brief job description: Restaurant Manager

Place of work: any hotel owned by Riverdale Hotels Ltd

Signed ………………….(employee)
Date:……………………..

Signed …………………..(employer)
Date……………………

Remember

There are different types of contract of employment but they should all include the same important features: job position, place of work, hours of work and rate of pay.

Activity

3   Lindsay has some questions about her job at the White Hart Hotel and her contract of employment. She is concerned that she could be asked to work at any hotel owned by Riverdale Hotels Ltd – will she be given enough time to prepare for a move to a different hotel? There is also the question of holidays; what does 'out of season' mean?

Discuss how the contract of employment could be changed to make the terms and conditions of Lindsay's employment clearer. Produce a revised version incorporating your changes.

Did you know ??????

According to the Department of Education and Employment only about 5.5 per cent of the UK workforce have temporary contracts.

Recruitment

There is a variety of reasons why a vacancy could arise in a business. For example:

- growth of the company
- promotion of job holder
- retirement or relocation of the job holder.

Whatever the reason, the HR department will take the steps shown in Figure A to find a new employee.

The first stage of this process, identifying the vacancy, is discussed in detail on pages 54–55.

Here, you are going to look at the third stage in this process when the business decides how to let potential candidates know about the vacancy.

Methods of recruitment

Internal recruitment means filling the position by promoting, retraining or relocating somebody who already works for the business. Vacancies can be advertised on notice boards, in a newsletter or on the company intranet (see Chapter 8).

B

Advantages of internal recruitment	Disadvantages of internal recruitment
Time – the vacancy can be filled quickly	Choice – limited range of possible candidates
Cost – there is no need for expensive advertising	Replacement – promotion creates another vacancy
Knowledge – the business is aware of the abilities and potential of the candidate	New ideas – an opportunity to bring in a fresh approach might be lost

External

External recruitment means looking for a candidate from outside the business. The choice of which method to use will depend on the type of vacancy. If the work is low-skilled then local recruitment will be sufficient. Where the job requires a high level of qualifications and experience, it is more likely that the methods chosen will cover a wider area – national or even international.

Notice boards: outside the business showing current vacancies. It is difficult to include a lot of detail and this method will require a lot of support material giving all the necessary information. It is most successful where there are a lot of passers-by.

Job Centre Plus: run by the government, this offers free recruitment services online and in job centres throughout the UK.

Objective

Understand the process of recruiting staff.

Identify the vacancy

|

Write an advertisement

|

Advertise the position

|

Shortlist candidates

|

Select the best candidate for the position

A *The steps involved in selecting and recruiting a new employee*

Key terms

Internal recruitment: filling vacancies from within the business through promotion, retraining or relocation.

External recruitment: using means outside the company to advertise vacancies.

Did you know ??????

Many businesses now offer financial incentives to employees who recommend a person to fill a vacancy. If the new recruit stays for more than an agreed period of time (e.g. one year) the employee who recommended them receives a cash bonus.

∞links

Find out more at **www.jobcentreplus.gov.uk**

Agencies: **recruitment agencies** are specialist organisations that charge firms for help with recruiting the best employees. They work at a local and national level. The fees charged can be quite high so agencies are often used for senior posts or when other methods have failed to find a suitable candidate.

Newspapers: the local newspaper is often a very successful method of recruitment for lower-skilled jobs. For more highly skilled work and management positions, national newspapers are more likely to be effective in attracting high-quality applicants.

Trade press: this method is very useful to target potential candidates with specific skills and experience.

Internet: there are a huge number of websites specifically designed to help with recruitment. Businesses can also use their own websites to advertise for jobs.

C

Advantages of external recruitment	Disadvantages of external recruitment
Range: a wider choice is available to the business, so it is more likely to get the best candidate	Cost: it can be very expensive to advertise vacancies, even at a local level
Ideas: new approaches and 'fresh eyes' can help the firm gain an advantage over rivals	Time: it might take longer to fill a vacancy, which slows down the progress of the business

Riverdale Hotels Ltd

Case study

The White Hart Hotel in Somerset wants to recruit a restaurant manager. The HR department has decided to advertise the position internally first because there are a number of assistant restaurant managers within the company who have the experience and qualities required for the job. However, in each case it would involve a move of over 50 miles which could put some candidates off. Riverdale Hotels would also consider recruiting candidates from Somerset as well as people from the European Union wishing to work in the UK.

Activities

Use the information in the case study to answer the following questions:

1 Describe the recruitment process the HR department at Riverdale Hotels should follow to appoint the new restaurant manager.

2 Briefly describe the possible methods of recruitment that Riverdale Hotels Ltd could use to recruit a restaurant manager.

3 Use your knowledge and judgement to recommend the most suitable method of recruitment. Justify your choice.

There are many reasons for a job vacancy but the duties of the job holder and the type of person best suited to the work can change due, for example, to technological advances or reorganisation.

A **job description** gives the job title, what the job involves, who the job holder reports to and who they are responsible for.

Riverdale Hotels

The HR department has drawn up a job description and **person specification** for the restaurant manager post at the White Hart Hotel in Somerset.

Job description for restaurant manager:

- To ensure all costs are maintained within budget.
- To lead and motivate the restaurant team in providing the highest possible standard of customer care and service.
- To manage the restaurant staff rota and the routine cleaning schedule.
- To maintain accurate records of all liquor stocks held in the restaurant.
- To attend weekly briefing meetings with the general manager.

Person specification for restaurant manager:

- At least three years' previous relevant experience.
- Excellent communication skills.
- Good attention to detail.
- Must possess excellent interpersonal skills.
- Excellent team working and self-management skills.
- Must have 'can do' attitude, be flexible and self-motivated.
- Proven passion in customer service.
- Willingness to work unsocial hours.

From these documents the following advertisement was published on an online hospitality recruitment site:

> **Restaurant manager required for prestigious hotel in Somerset**
>
> A fantastic opportunity to join The White Hart Hotel, part of Riverdale Hotels Ltd, as restaurant manager.
>
> An elegant hotel, located in the heart of Somerset, The White Hart provides a perfect base for weekend breaks or short sightseeing trips whilst enjoying comfortable up-market accommodation and facilities.
>
> Reporting to the general manager, we are looking for a candidate with restaurant experience or a restaurant manager looking to get into the hotel industry.
>
> The restaurant manager will be focusing on the 60-seat restaurant serving breakfast, conference lunches and an à la carte menu, as well as other duties within the hotel.

Objectives

Understand the content of a job description.

Understand the content of a person specification.

Key terms

Job description: the job title, brief details of duties, who the job holder reports to and who they are responsible for.

Person specification: the skills, qualifications, experience and personal qualities of the ideal candidate.

Activity

1. Go online and find the website for a business you might like to work for in the future. Find the section that gives details of career opportunities and read about the options open to you. Prepare a short report about the recruitment process used by this company. Include the following elements:

   - How many ways can you apply?
   - How do you think the business will select candidates?
   - Is it clear what skills, experience and qualifications candidates need?
   - Is the online application form easy to complete?

Applications

Once the job has been advertised, people will start to apply, either by completing an application form by hand or online, or by sending a **curriculum vitae (CV)** with a covering letter explaining why they are suited to the job. Sometimes both methods are used.

Short-listing

If there are a lot of applicants for a job, the firm will have to select the most suitable people for the next stage in the process, an interview. A short-list form identifies the essential and desirable requirements for the job. In the White Hart Hotel example, restaurant experience was essential and management experience desirable.

Key terms

Curriculum vitae (CV): a summary of a person's education and work experience.

AQA Examiner's tip

You must be very clear about the difference between a job description and a person specification.

Activity

2   Look at the following CVs which were sent in response to the restaurant manager vacancy at the White Hart Hotel. Rank the applicants in order of suitability for the post and explain your choice.

Applicant 1

Name: Carlos Millet
Date of birth: 10.12.1968

Employment history:
1986–1996 Riviera Hotel, Barcelona, Spain
1996–2000 Mountain Hotel, Saltzburg, Austria
2000–2008 Clogs Hotel, Amsterdam, Holland

Qualifications:
College Certificate, St Joseph's School, Barcelona, Spain

Applicant 2

Name: Philip Evans
Date of birth: 04.03.1976

Employment history:
1992–1996 Pratt's Restaurant, Bridgwater, Somerset
1996–1998 Jones' Restaurant, Bridgwater
1998–2001 High Grove Hotel, Bridgwater
2001–2008 Regency Hotel, Bridgwater

Qualifications:
3 GCSEs at grade C or above
NVQ Level 2 in Hospitality and catering

Applicant 3

Name: Marian Jones
Date of birth: 07.07.1980

Employment history:
1998–2004 Oliver's Restaurant, Cambridge
2004–2008 Newton's Hotel, Cambridge

Qualifications:
5 GCSEs at grade C or higher including maths and English
NVQ Level 3 in Hospitality and customer care

A

Employment rights and responsibilities

There are laws designed to make sure that people have a right to be treated fairly during the recruitment and selection for a job and once they are doing that job. They can be grouped under the term **equal opportunities**, which means that everyone should be treated equally and given an equal chance at work, whatever their gender, race, age, religious beliefs and whether or not they have a disability.

The Sex Discrimination Act

This Act is designed to make sure that men and women are treated equally in the workplace. This means that:

- a job cannot be advertised as 'woman wanted to …' (apart from a few exceptions such as a job as a personal carer)
- candidates for a job should not be discriminated against because of their gender, by the way they are questioned or treated during an interview
- men and women should not be treated differently when training or promotion opportunities arise
- gender should not be a reason for 'sacking' someone.

The Equal Pay Act

This law was passed to make sure that men and women are paid the same for 'like work'. The difficulty sometimes is proving what 'like work' is. Coventry City Council has had to deal with claims of **discrimination** under the Equal Pay Act. Care workers and cooks claimed that their work was equal to that of refuse collectors and other male manual workers who enjoyed generous bonuses.

The National Minimum Wage also ensures that employees are paid what is seen as the minimum hourly rate which it is acceptable to pay someone. It is reviewed regularly and there is a rate for 18–21 year olds and another higher rate for those aged 22 or over. Find out what the minimum wage is for both age groups.

Race Relations Act

This Act makes it illegal to discriminate against someone because of their:

- race
- colour
- national origin
- ethnic origin.

This applies to all aspects of employing someone, from recruitment, selection, training, promotion opportunities and terminating or ending someone's employment. This means that the best person for a job must be chosen, based on what they can do, not where they come from or the colour of their skin.

Objectives

Be aware of current laws about employment rights and responsibilities.

Understand how they affect a business.

Key terms

Equal opportunities: the principle that everyone should be treated equally, whatever their race, gender, age or level of disability when being recruited, selected, trained, paid and promoted at work.

Discrimination: treating someone differently because of their gender, race, disability or age.

A *People must be chosen for a job based on what they can do, not where they come from or the colour of their skin*

The Disability Discrimination Act

This Act tries to ensure that people with disabilities are not refused employment in a certain place of work because of their disability. A workplace which employs more than 20 people must give equal opportunity to job applicants who have disabilities. They must also make sure that the workplace is suitable for them to carry out their work. The employer is expected to make 'reasonable adjustments' to the workplace to accommodate someone with a disability. This means building a ramp for a wheelchair user or installing equipment to help someone with a hearing difficulty.

Employment equality (age) regulations

These regulations are to make sure that people are not discriminated against or overlooked for jobs, training or education because of their age. Some businesses now have a policy to actively try to recruit workers over the age of 65. Sainsbury's does this and has also removed the box for 'age' on its application forms. DIY store B&Q has no set retirement age and actively tries to recruit people of different ages. It has found many benefits to this, such as less absence from work and a lower turnover of staff.

> **Case study**
>
> ### Teacher wins indirect age discrimination claim
>
> It has been decided that advertising for a relatively new teacher to save costs was discriminating against older teachers. A teaching job advertised by Milton Keynes council said that it would be suitable for someone in the 'first five years of their career'. An applicant, Ms Rainbow, with 34 years' teaching experience was not short-listed for the job. It was decided by a tribunal that the advertisement was indirectly discriminating against older teachers as there was no evidence that the council could not afford to employ a more experienced teacher.
>
> Do you think that the council should have been able to advertise for a teacher in the 'first five years of their career'? Think about both sides of the argument.

Activities

1. Check your knowledge of these regulations by making a leaflet for someone responsible for recruiting, selecting and training new employees. The leaflet should look attractive and be easy to read. It should contain the essential legal information this person would need to know.

2. Research cases of businesses that have been found guilty of breaking some of the laws discussed here. Think about why so many businesses seem to break these laws. Useful sources of information are **www.ageconcern.org.uk**, **www.bbc.co.uk** then search for 'discrimination'.

> **Did you know** ??????
>
> A survey carried out in 2007 by the charity Leonard Cheshire Disability found that four in ten disabled workers have experienced discrimination or prejudice at work. The survey also found that 18 per cent felt that they had been overlooked for promotion because of their disability.

Calling time on age discrimination

A mini-guide to age discrimination at work

B *Age Concern campaign for the rights of older employees*

> **AQA   Examiner's tip**
>
> You do not need detailed knowledge such as the dates of these Acts, but you need to know the main principles of the laws. You might need to apply them to a business situation in an examination question and understand how the laws affect what the business can and cannot do.

5

In this chapter you have learnt:

- ✔ the process of recruiting and selecting staff
- ✔ the content of a job description and a person specification
- ✔ the forms that a contract of employment may take
- ✔ the main features of a contract of employment
- ✔ employment rights and responsibilities.

Revision questions

1 Decide whether each of the following statements is true or false.

a A job description details the tasks and duties of a job role.

b A job advertisement is written before a vacancy is identified.

c A company intranet is an external method of recruitment.

d Internal recruitment is normally cheaper than external recruitment.

e A curriculum vitae gives a summary of a person's education and work experience.

f Not all employees are entitled to a contract of employment.

g A temporary contract continues indefinitely.

h A job centre is not an external method of recruitment.

i The skills, qualifications and experience required for a job are included in a description specification.

j A full-time employee normally works 37.5 hours per week.

Case study

Peng Trading

Peng Trading imports a range of clothes and accessories aimed at the teenage market, which it sells through an online store. The business has grown very quickly and the owners, Husham El Sheik and Jason Tien, want to open their first shop in Birmingham. They need to recruit a full-time shop manager and six part-time sales assistants. Husham and Jason are also keen to employ a human resources manager so they can spend more time abroad sourcing new suppliers. They have drawn up job descriptions and person specifications for all the vacancies and are considering the best methods of recruiting and selecting suitable candidates. Jason and Husham are unclear about the types of contract of employment they might need and what the most important features are.

Activities

1 Explain the difference between a job description and a person specification.

2 Identify two methods of external recruitment Peng Trading could use to recruit the shop manager. In each case explain one possible advantage and disadvantage to the business.

3 Explain why Husham and Jason will need to use different contracts of employment for the sales assistants and the human resources manager.

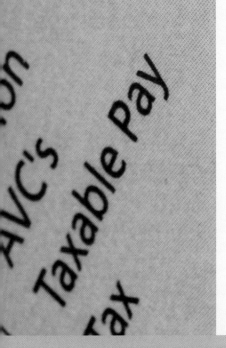

6 Training and rewarding staff

In this chapter

6.1 Methods of training employees

6.2 Ways of paying staff

6.3 Rewards other than pay

The recruitment of new staff is just the beginning of the responsibility of the HR department; this chapter looks at how employees can be trained and rewarded.

▮ Did you know?

A survey by *The Guardian* found that in 2007 the head of Barclays investment bank received more than £21m in salary and bonuses. The Royal Bank of Scotland's chief executive was paid £5.4m, including bonuses.

Orange runs a three-week induction programme for new contact centre staff. There is a mixture of instructor-led workshops and eLearning covering brand awareness, product and systems training and customer service skills for 10–12 new employees at a time.

According to the Citizens Advice Bureau a company car, a petrol allowance, subsidised meals and medical insurance are among the most common fringe benefits offered at work.

Riverdale Hotels Ltd

The White Hart Hotel in Somerset is one of the 12 hotels run by Riverdale Hotels Ltd. It has 56 en suite bedrooms offering a very high standard of accommodation. The South West Restaurant has a menu reflecting the seasonal produce available in the area as well as an extensive and imaginative wine list. The new restaurant manager, appointed in Chapter 5, has joined the team at the White Hart. Her training needs will be considered in Chapter 6.

Case study

6.1 Methods of training employees

Training is a very important activity which involves both new and experienced employees.

Induction training is for new staff and must include health and safety at work. It is also likely to include information about the business. This type of training varies in length but should make the new recruit feel at ease about starting work. Induction training might include short film presentations and the use of a 'buddy' system where existing employees look after new recruits and show them how everything works.

Activity

1. Make a list of all the information a pupil should receive when they start school or college. Use this to prepare a four-page induction booklet to be issued to all new students. The booklet could include:

   - health and safety rules (e.g. no running in corridors)
   - fire drill (e.g. a log to show evidence that the pupil has taken part in a fire practice)
   - dress code
   - facts about the school/college (e.g. a brief history).

Methods of training

In-house training happens at the normal place of work and might include the following features:

- being shown how to complete tasks or learn new skills by an experienced member of staff
- working at a slower pace until the necessary skills are learnt
- working with new machinery or equipment
- working alongside existing employees, watching what they do.

A

Advantages of in-house training	Disadvantages of in-house training
Cheap – no travel costs	Takes trainers away from their normal job
New employee gets to meet colleagues and settles in quickly	Trainers can teach bad habits
Training can include all the skills needed to do a particular job and 'how it is done here'	An employee who is good at their job might not be good at demonstrating or explaining the work to a new recruit

External/off-the-job training takes employees away from their normal place of work and may include the following features:

- being instructed by specialists provided by another business at a training centre
- day release from work to attend a local college
- working with employees from other branches of the same company or workers from other businesses.

Objectives

Understand that employees can be trained both in house and externally.

Be able to choose the best method of training to fit a particular situation.

Key terms

Induction training: training to help new employees settle in to the business.

In-house training: happens at the place of work.

External/off-the-job training: happens away from the place of work.

Did you know ??????

The North Lincolnshire Council Ranger Service has an induction programme for its volunteers which includes:

- an assigned coordinator
- a site map and tour of the site including an introduction to other staff
- a chart showing the staff structure
- a health and safety talk (e.g. fire exits, first aid locations, use of the radio, use of the telephone; the use of identity badges on site).

Source: www.volunteering.org.uk

Did you know ??????

Nippy Taxis of Scarborough put 50 drivers and directors through NVQ Level 2 in Road Passenger Transport. Staff completed their coursework round their shifts and met with external assessors once a week.

Source: Train to gain

B

Advantages of off-the-job training	Disadvantages of off-the-job training
Experts can be used	Travel costs can make it expensive
Trainees can learn the correct method, make mistakes and practise without affecting the quality of goods or service provided by the business	While being trained the employee is not productive
There is less pressure to learn quickly which should reduce mistakes	Trainees are not learning to work as part of the team they will eventually be part of

The role of the HR department is to select the most appropriate method of training for any given situation. For businesses that tend to recruit a lot of people at the same time, in-house induction training makes sense, whereas for other firms where new recruits are spread over a number of sites (e.g. fast-food outlets) it makes more sense to organise induction at a regional centre.

Case study

Riverdale Hotels

The new restaurant manager, Lindsay Hamilton, is joining a group of new recruits to Riverdale Hotels Ltd for a day of induction training. This will introduce her to the values of the business and the vision of the owners. It is also an opportunity to meet other employees of the group on an informal basis. The training is held at the headquarters in Leicestershire.

The most important aspect of the training is to ensure that all new recruits will offer the high level of service that has made Riverdale Hotels so successful in a very competitive market. There are a lot of group activities and role-play exercises to ensure that everyone understands the importance of keeping customers happy.

On her arrival at the White Hart Hotel, Lindsay has another day of induction training covering the practical knowledge she will need to fulfil her role. She has the opportunity to meet most of her team and the manager she will report to.

Activity

2 Using your knowledge and the information in the case study, design an induction programme for new recruits to Riverdale Hotels Ltd. This should include one day at the headquarters in Leicestershire and one day at the hotel where the new recruit is employed. Select from the following options:

- Health and safety talk and video
- Company history, values and vision
- Structure of the organisation
- Tour of hotel
- Meet the staff
- Team-building exercises.

Make sure that you explain clearly why you have included each element of the induction training programme.

Did you know ??????

Travel company Thomas Cook's overseas resort staff receive an eight-day residential induction in the UK, followed by 6–12 days' on-the-job training at the resort.

AQA Examiner's tip

Make sure that you can choose the right method of training for a given situation.

∞links

The government is very keen to promote training within business. Find out more at www.traintogain.gov.uk

Remember

There are financial costs to training both direct (e.g. paying the trainer) and indirect (e.g. working time lost while the employee is being trained). These costs must be taken into consideration when deciding on the most suitable form of training.

∞links

More information about induction training can be found at www.cipd.co.uk

6.2 Ways of paying staff

Methods of payment

There is a variety of methods of paying employees depending on the type of work they do:

- **Wages** are given as an hourly rate (e.g. £6 per hour) and employees are normally paid weekly.

- **Salaries** are quoted as a yearly (annual) figure (e.g. £16,000 p.a. (per annum)) and are paid monthly on a date specified in the contract of employment (see pages 50–51).

In both cases the payment is likely to be made directly into a bank account for security reasons.

- **Overtime** is paid when work cannot be completed during normal working hours and is often paid at a higher rate such as time and a half (e.g. £9 per hour instead of £6). Overtime tends to be paid to employees paid a wage rather than a salary.

- **Bonus payments** are made if a particular target is achieved (e.g. increase profit by 10 per cent). A bonus can be paid to an individual employee or to everyone in the company.

A *A John Lewis store*

- **Commission** is additional money paid to an employee when an item is sold. It is normally a percentage of the value of the sale (e.g. if a sofa sells for £800 and the commission is 15 per cent, then the sales assistant will receive an extra £120 on top of their normal pay). This is a good way of encouraging employees to try to make as many sales as possible.

Objectives

Understand the different methods of paying an employee.

Be able to identify situations when different methods are used.

Key terms

Wage: quoted at an hourly rate and paid weekly.

Salary: quoted at an annual rate and paid monthly.

Overtime: extra pay for working longer than normal hours, often a higher rate than normal pay.

Bonus: extra money for achieving a specific target, often paid annually.

Commission: extra money received for making a sale, normally a percentage of the value of the sale.

Did you know ??????

Early in 2008, the John Lewis Partnership announced it was giving a bonus payment to employees (known as partners) of 20 per cent of their salary or ten weeks' pay. Find out more about this by going to www.johnlewispartnership.co.uk.

Activity

1 Match the worker with the best method of payment. In each case explain your choice.

Worker	Method of payment
Nurse	Basic salary plus commission
Bricklayer	Salary
Cleaner	Salary plus bonus
Double glazing sales person	Wage
Senior manager	Wage plus overtime

Riverdale Hotels Ltd

Lindsay Hamilton, the new restaurant manager at the White Hart Hotel in Somerset, has just received her first pay slip. She knows that she did no overtime, although she does receive a 10 per cent bonus if she can get a company booking for a function such as a Christmas party. Lindsay understands that her salary of £1,500 per month (£18,000 per year) will be reduced because she has to pay income tax and National Insurance contributions.

Here is an example of a pay slip for Lindsay Hamilton.

Pay slip   **Riverdale Hotels Ltd**   Month Ending 30 September 2008

Employee: Lindsay Hamilton   Employee Number: 1067   Tax Code: 612L

PAYMENTS	£	DEDUCTIONS	£
Basic Pay	1500	Income Tax	240
Bonus	100	National Insurance	120
Total Gross Pay	1600	Total Deductions	360

Net Pay (Gross Pay minus Total Deductions) **£1240**

Activity

2 In the following month Lindsay works eight hours overtime and arranges two Christmas parties. She receives 10 per cent of the value of each party as a bonus.

   ■ Overtime is paid at £12 per hour.

   ■ One Christmas booking is worth £300 and the other is worth £600.

   Calculate:

   a Lindsay's overtime pay for the month

   b the total bonus payment she will receive for the month.

Remember

Net pay = gross pay minus deductions.

Did you know ??????

Student loan repayments become a deduction from pay once a person starts to earn more than a certain amount per year. In 2008 this was £15,000.

Case study

6.3 Rewards other than pay

There are other ways of rewarding employees for their work and commitment to the business that do not appear on a pay slip; these are known as **fringe benefits**. They have a financial value. Here are some of the most common fringe benefits:

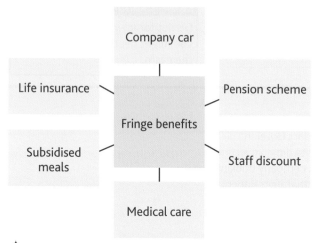

Company car

Life insurance

Pension scheme

Fringe benefits

Subsidised meals

Staff discount

Medical care

A *Common fringe benefits*

Diagram **A** shows that fringe benefits have very different financial values; a company car might be worth a lot more than a subsidised canteen or staff discount to an individual employee. Senior managers tend to receive the most valuable fringe benefits offered by a business. This is because they are more difficult to replace and are likely to have very specialised skills and bring a wide range of benefits to the business.

The aim is to find out which benefits will attract the highest quality employee. For example:

- A tax professional might be offered a pension, private healthcare, 25 days holiday and free parking.
- An insurance sales specialist could be offered a company pension scheme, childcare vouchers and 33 days annual leave.
- A sales assistant in a major high-street retail store might receive 20 per cent discount on products.

Objectives

Be aware of other ways of rewarding employees, in addition to payment.

Key terms

Fringe benefit: additional reward given to some or all employees.

Did you know ??????

Employees at Marks & Spencer and B&Q get a 20 per cent discount on all goods.

Source: jobs.trovit.co.uk

AQA Examiner's tip

Not all fringe benefits will be suitable for every job. Think carefully about which are likely to be offered by a particular business.

Activity

1 Use the internet and local newspapers to search for a range of job opportunities in your area. Make a display of your findings showing the different fringe benefits offered to potential candidates. From this display investigate whether there are any relationships between level of pay, experience, qualifications and the types of fringe benefits offered.

Did you know ??????

BUPA Health Insurance provides private healthcare to around 13,000 employees of entertainment and communications company Virgin Media.

Source: www.easier.com

Case study

Riverdale Hotels Ltd

The senior management of the company are meeting to decide what benefits should be offered to existing and future staff employed at the hotels in the group. At the moment they all get the same – a discount when staying at any hotel within the group and free meals while on duty. Recently a few candidates for senior positions have turned job offers down because the fringe benefits offered have not been as good as they expected. Among the options to be considered are private healthcare, a company pension scheme and use of the hotel's leisure facilities.

The benefits Riverdale Hotels Ltd hope to gain include attracting high-quality staff and retaining good employees who might otherwise be tempted away by rival hotels on the lookout for experienced staff to improve their standard of service.

However, there are costs involved: paying for the private healthcare or contributing to the company pension scheme.

The senior managers have to decide whether all staff or those above a certain managerial level should be given more fringe benefits.

Activities

2   Identify one additional fringe benefit that could be offered to:

- a head chef
- a junior receptionist
- a hotel manager.

Justify your choice.

3   What fringe benefits would you offer to a restaurant manager?

4   Explain why the fringe benefits offered to staff within the hotel chain are likely to vary.

Remember

All fringe benefits have a financial cost and benefit to a business.

Did you know ??????

Most public sector employees (nurses, teachers, local authority workers, etc.) do not receive any fringe benefits.

B *Chef*

C *Receptionist*

D *Hotel manager*

In this chapter you have learnt:

✔ methods of training employees both in house and externally

✔ different methods of paying an employee and the situations when they are used

✔ ways of rewarding employees in addition to payment.

Revision questions

Select the best answer for each question.

1 An example of in-house training is:

a observing alongside existing employees, watching what they do

b attending college to gain a diploma qualification

c going to a specialist training centre to learn management skills.

2 Which of the following is **not** an advantage of off-the-job training?

a Trainees can learn the correct method, make mistakes and practise without affecting the quality of goods or service provided by the business.

b Travel costs can make it expensive.

c There is less pressure to learn quickly, which should reduce mistakes.

3 Overtime is:

a paid at the same rate as normal hours

b often paid at a higher rate such as time and a half (e.g. £9 per hour instead of £6)

c paid as a lump sum, normally at Christmas.

4 An employee is to receive a bonus of 2 per cent of her salary of £23,000 per year. She will receive an extra:

a £4,600

b £400

c £460.

5 Which of the following is not an example of fringe benefits?

a a subsidised canteen

b medical insurance

c a Christmas bonus.

Case study

Peng Trading

Husham and Jason have recruited all the new members of staff and are planning the induction training which is to be held at the head office where the existing three full-time and four part-time staff work. The shop manager and the human resources manager are to be paid an annual salary, while the part-time sales assistants are on an hourly rate and will be paid a weekly wage. Jason is keen to offer the sales staff commission and the human resources manager a bonus if the business profits increase, but Husham is not convinced; he thinks it would be better to offer fringe benefits to all employees.

Activities

1 Explain what induction training is and why it is beneficial to employees and employers.

2 Explain the difference between a wage and a salary.

3 Use appropriate examples to explain the kind of fringe benefits Husham might want to offer:

a the part-time employees at the new shop and the head office

b the human resources manager.

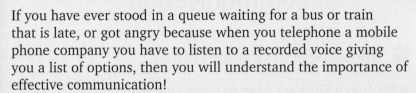

7 Communication

In this chapter

7.1	The purpose and importance of communication
7.2	Communication systems
7.3	Choosing the right medium
7.4	Barriers to communication

If you have ever stood in a queue waiting for a bus or train that is late, or got angry because when you telephone a mobile phone company you have to listen to a recorded voice giving you a list of options, then you will understand the importance of effective communication!

Developments in technology should make it easier for businesses to communicate with all their stakeholders: suppliers; customers; employees; the community; the government; banks.

However, it is not as straightforward as it seems and this chapter considers the issues.

Throughout this chapter the following case study will be used:

Case study

Evolution Barbers

'Alex Kamintzis is a hairdresser who had always worked for other people but really wanted to branch out on his own.

Unfortunately he discovered that he could not afford to set up a salon: the cost of renting a property and equipping it fully was beyond his means.'

Source: news.bbc.co.uk

To realise his dream Alex decided to go mobile. To begin with he worked three days a week in a town-centre salon. He bought a large van which had been kitted out as a salon and began to find customers on business parks in the Watford area on the other two days.

Now he works full time in his mobile salon and is hoping to employ another stylist in the near future.

Alex has to keep a close eye on his business costs which are very different from those of ordinary salons.

Alex also has a business partner who looks after the administration, finance and marketing of the business. There are many jobs that need regular attention while Alex is busy cutting hair:

- *Suppliers:* paying invoices ordering new stocks of hair care products; arranging delivery of new stocks.
- *Customers:* negotiating new business opportunities; promoting the business to potential clients; collating feedback from the website.
- *Finance:* keeping track of the cash flow; banking money from cash sales; negotiating finance for possible expansion plans; recording all financial transactions.
- *Insurance:* negotiating appropriate insurance cover for the business.

Activity

Go to the website **www.evolutionbarbers.co.uk** for more information and to watch the BBC 2 video of an interview with Alex.

The purpose and importance of communication

◼ The purpose of communication

Why does a business need to communicate?

- To gain **information** or data from sources inside and outside the business.
- To pass on information or data to others inside and outside the business.

What is internal communication?

This is information and data passed between people within one business.

1. Communication between members of a **team** (e.g. sales representatives working in the marketing department)

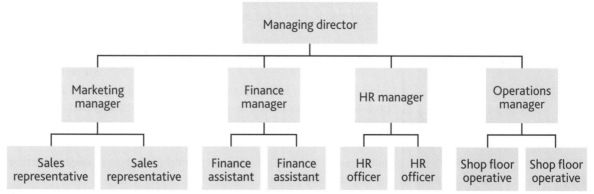

A *Communication between employees at different levels of the hierarchy in an organisation*

The sales representatives in a sales team might communicate sales data or information about business contacts.

2. Communication between different levels in the hierarchy of the business

Diagram **A** shows a hierarchical business structure where communication tends to be vertical. Employees share information and data with others in their department or one level up or down the hierarchy.

3. Communication between departments within the business

If a business is going to operate successfully and achieve its goals, all departments need to know what the others are doing.

What is external communication?

External communication takes place between:

1. a business and its suppliers
2. a business and its customers or clients
3. a business and other stakeholder groups.

B *Communication between the members of a sales team*

Activity

1 Consider these pictures. What image and tone do they convey and how effective do you think they are?

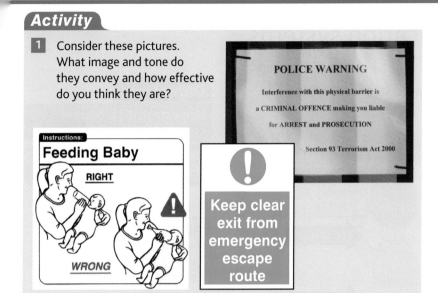

The importance of communication

In good communication the information or data should have the following features:

- it must be clear
- it must be accurate
- it must create the image and tone the business wants to convey.

If information is not passed from the sender to the recipient properly, problems might arise.

- It might be misunderstood.
- It might be misleading.
- It might be misinterpreted.

The benefits of effective communication

If a business takes into consideration who it is communicating with and how it communicates, there are several benefits:

1 Well-informed employees are likely to be motivated because they feel that they are an important part of the organisation. This should lead to improved customer service which improves the image of the business and helps it achieve its objectives.

2 Customers who are well informed about products and who feel that their opinions are important are more likely to become loyal to a particular brand and buy other products from the same company.

3 Suppliers want to know about the requirements of their customers, when orders will arrive and when they will be paid. If this information is easily available and they have direct contact with their customers, they are much more likely to provide high-quality supplies that meet the specifications of their customers.

If employees, customers and suppliers are happy, then the business is much more likely to achieve its objectives, be that increased market share or higher profit margins.

Did you know

Virgin Atlantic wanted to pass on information about special offers to its customers more quickly. Emailing was often blocked by spam filters so it created a service called Virgin Atlantic Alerts. Customers download an application which sends details of special deals directly to the customer's desktop. Over 4,000 customers downloaded the application in the first two months.

Source: www.skinkers.com

Did you know

Starbucks Coffee Company, a very successful business, allows employees (called partners) the opportunity to get involved in the business through 'Partner Blend'. Employees elect representatives across all Starbucks, who meet with the UK leadership team two or three times a year to discuss how the business is developing.

AQA **Examiner's tip**

Think about businesses whose communications you are familiar with, for example:

- school/college
- Connexions
- mobile phone network provider.

What do they say about the business?

Activity

2 Use all the information available about Evolution Barbers to create an A3 display including text and images to show why communication is important to this business and the benefits it brings Alex and his partner.

7.2 Communication systems

How to get the message across effectively

The process of communication

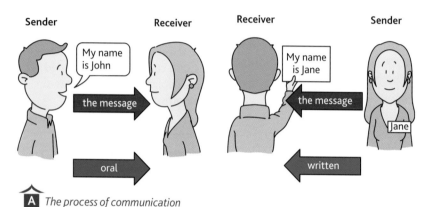

Sender — Receiver — Receiver — Sender

My name is John

the message

oral

My name is Jane

Jane

the message

written

A *The process of communication*

In any communication it is important to identify the sender, the receiver(s), the message and the **medium** (e.g. printed publication, post, telecommunications, face-to-face).

The sender has to decide the best way to transfer the information to the receiver so that the message is understood.

Channels of communication

Formal/informal

In some cases information needs to be formally recorded because it might be needed in the future. This includes invoices, minutes of meetings, audit reports and legal documents such as contracts of employment.

In other situations a more informal approach is possible. Telephone conversations, e-mails, text messages and face-to-face discussions are generally thought of as being informal ways of communicating.

Internal/external

Internal communication is restricted to employees within an organisation or department. External communication includes one or more of the stakeholder groups associated with the business.

Confidential/non-confidential

Confidential means that the information or data is restricted to a certain number of recipients. Non-confidential means that the communication is for general release and can be shared with others within and outside the business.

Objectives

Understand the process of communication.

Understand the different channels of communication.

Key terms

Medium: a way of communicating any information or data for any purpose.

Confidential: information or data only available to people with authorised access.

links

For more detail on choosing the right medium see pages 72–73.

B *Minutes are a written record of a meeting*

Urgent/non-urgent

A communication marked urgent means that the information or data received requires immediate attention. On the other hand, a communication marked non-urgent might just be for information rather than action.

◼ Which method to choose

The options for communication methods available to a business are:

- oral
- visual
- written
- pictorial.

The following factors should be taken into consideration:

- the content of the message
- the audience.

Consider this situation: a company wants to give details of its sales figures to the whole workforce. Should they produce a report giving details of the figures or create graphical images to show the information in pictorial form?

In this case the graph is a better choice because the data is easier to understand for a non-specialist audience.

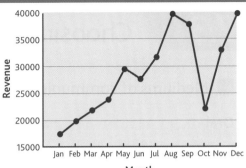

	A	B
1	**Month**	**Revenue**
2	Jan	$17,400
3	Feb	$19,800
4	Mar	$21,800
5	Apr	$23,800
6	May	$29,600
7	Jun	$27,600
8	Jul	$31,800
9	Aug	$39,700
10	Sep	$37,800
11	Oct	$21,900
12	Nov	$32,900
13	Dec	$39,800

C *A sales data spreadsheet and a graph of the same data*

Activity

3 Decide which method of communication is the most appropriate in the following situations. Make sure that you can justify your choice.

a   A customer complains that an employee has been rude and abusive to them on the telephone. You must inform the employee of the complaint.

b   Sales representatives throughout Europe must be informed urgently about a safety problem with a product they sell.

c   A delivery from a supplier 20 miles away is four hours late.

AQA *Examiner's tip*

It is important that you can explain clearly why you have selected a particular method of communication.

Case study

Evolution Barbers

Alex and his business partner at Evolution Barbers communicate on a daily basis about a whole range of issues. They send messages to and receive them from each other, suppliers, customers and business contacts such as the bank. Alex has noticed that sometimes misunderstandings arise and this slows down the completion of some work.

Activities

1 Use the case study to draw a diagram to illustrate the process of communication.

2 From the following list decide which channel of communication and which method of communicating would get the message across most effectively:

a   Alex needs to get evidence that he has permission to park his van on the business park he visits on a Monday within one month.

b   An e-mail has been received from a customer asking about the products used in the salon.

c   Alex needs to let his business partner know that he wants to take a week's holiday next month.

Make sure that you can justify the channels you have chosen.

Choosing the right medium

▪ Mediums of communication

Oral

- *Telephone calls:* to colleagues, customers and suppliers. Mobile phones mean that employees working remotely can stay in touch with head office. Other uses include call centres and business reception desks.
- *Face-to-face:* formal meetings with an **agenda** and **minutes**, informal meetings such as casual conversations, interviews, appraisals and presentations. Body language plays an important part in this type of communication.
- *Teleconferencing:* allows people in different locations to have a conversation. Phone lines are linked together so that each person can be heard.

Advantage

Instant feedback so problems can be dealt with immediately.

Disadvantage

The sender and receiver might speak different languages and it might be difficult to keep an accurate record of the discussion.

Visual

- *Video conferencing:* uses video cameras or webcams to enable people in different locations to see and hear each other during a discussion.
- *Electronic notice boards:* enable a business to display and update information for employees and customers via its computer system. The screen can be plasma or LCD and can be used within an organisation and externally.
- *PowerPoint presentations:* this software enables slides of text, graphs and images to be shown on a laptop or via a projector. The company name and logo as well as different font sizes and styles can be included in the presentation, which can be used many times and adapted easily for a different audience.

Advantage

IA lot of time can be saved on travel (video conferencing), updating information (electronic notice boards) or presentation preparation (PowerPoint presentations).

Disadvantages

If any part of the electronic system fails, is faulty or incompatible, then the medium cannot be used (all); the cost might be beyond the means of small and medium-sized businesses (video conferencing).

Objectives

Be able to choose a particular medium for communicating a message to the receiver.

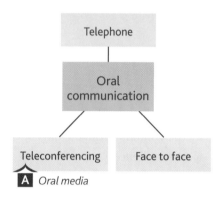

A *Oral media*

Key terms

Agenda: details of what is to be discussed at a future meeting.

Minutes: written records of meetings for future reference.

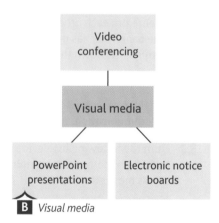

B *Visual media*

AQA Examiner's tip

Knowing all the ways of communication is only part of your task – you must be able to choose the most appropriate medium and justify your choice.

Written

- *Memos:* internal communications that are less formal and usually shorter than a letter.
- *Letters:* formal internal or external communications using accepted formats and styles. A letter acts as a record of a communication and normally includes the date and a unique reference number.
- *Financial documents:* formal standardised communications used to record and track the purchase and sale of goods and services.
- *Advertisements:* give information about products or vacancies in the company – businesses advertise locally, nationally and internationally.
- *E-mail messages:* allow text, graphs and pictures to be sent from one computer to another as long as the sender knows the receiver's e-mail address.
- *Text messages:* allow short messages and images to be transmitted very quickly.
- *Fax messages:* exact copies of text, graphics or images are sent from one machine to another via a telephone line.

Advantage
A record of the communication can be kept for future reference.

Disadvantage
The sender cannot be sure that the message reached the correct receiver and was interpreted correctly.

Graphical

- *Graphs and charts:* display data (e.g. sales figures) in a user-friendly way.
- *Production drawings:* technical drawings used to translate a designer's idea into reality.
- *Flow charts:* show the sequence of actions in a process to make it easier to understand.

Advantage
Non-specialists can access complex information.

Disadvantage
Graphical media are suitable for a limited range of communications.

Evolution Barbers

Alex is facing a number of problems while running his business.

1 He likes to visit the companies in each business park on a regular basis to encourage more employees to use the salon. However, it is getting more and more difficult to find the time as his business grows.

2 The number of firms advertising on the plasma screen in the salon is disappointing and needs to be increased.

3 Alex and his business partner must visit the bank and present a report on the business including sales figures and running costs. Alex only has a couple of hours to prepare for the appointment and does not want to read a lengthy written document.

4 He often thinks of things to tell his business partner, but forgets them by the time he gets back to the office. His partner writes messages received during the day on scraps of paper, which often get lost.

Activities

1 Choose a suitable medium for solving each of these communication problems facing Evolution Barbers.

2 Prepare a presentation to Evolution Barbers showing how the correct choice of media could solve its communication problems.

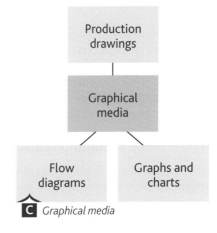

C *Graphical media*

Remember
There is a difference between **method** and **medium**.

7.4 Barriers to communication

■ Barriers to effective communication

Jargon

Jargon is technical language used by people in a specific industry or business as a kind of shorthand. The idea is that it speeds up communication with other people who are familiar with the terms. Jargon can also be used when one person is trying to mislead another or not really answer the problem or question they face. Here are some examples of business jargon.

- D-CAB is an industry term for digital cable.
- CAD means computer-aided design.
- Golden handcuffs: a series of rewards and penalties designed to try to stop an employee from leaving a business.
- Banana problem: one that somebody with little knowledge or experience could solve (e.g. a gorilla!).
- Snail mail: sending a communication by post (it is slower than electronic mail).

There have been many complaints about the use of jargon in business because it can lead to misunderstanding and frustration. If the receiver of a message does not understand the language used they could lose confidence and begin to mistrust the sender.

Noise

'Noise' refers to anything that disrupts the message as it is passed from the sender to the receiver. It includes background noise which makes it difficult for the receiver to hear an oral message. Factors such as poor lighting, faulty equipment, poor acoustics and bad office design can all interfere with the message, as can cultural differences and even the mood of the sender or receiver.

Poor choice of communication channel or medium

It is sometimes difficult to assess which channel of communication might be best. The sender of a message makes assumptions about the receiver:

1 The availability of compatible technology.
2 Their physical ability (sight, hearing).
3 Their ability to understand the language of the sender.

In the same way, the medium chosen could also be a mistake, for example using a mobile phone where there is no signal or circulating a memo containing sensitive information to everyone in a company.

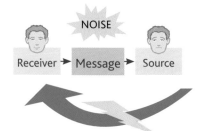

NOISE

Receiver → Message → Source

Feedback/changed behaviour

A *The impact of noise on communication*

Inappropriate presentation

An inappropriate presentation of the message could represent a barrier to communication because the intended audience might not be able to understand it. If the message is too complicated it might be ignored by the receiver, as sometimes happens with instruction manuals and user guides. PowerPoint presentations are particularly prone to this problem: slides contain too much information, change too quickly or are so stylised that the message is lost as words fly about the screen. On the other hand, the message might be over-simplified, which can be just as bad.

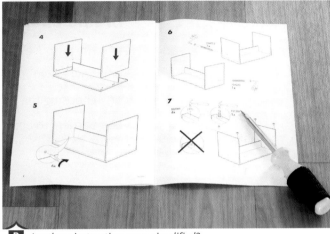

B *Are these instructions over-simplified?*

Activity

2 Use a desktop publishing package to produce an A4 leaflet for the double-glazing manufacturing industry. The leaflet should provide a guide to the effective use of the following three media when communicating with sales staff, customers and suppliers:

a mobile phone

b PowerPoint

c e-mail.

Evolution Barbers

Case study

Alex and his business partner have a monthly meeting on a Monday morning to discuss the progress of Evolution Barbers. At the next meeting they are going to talk about why some of their attempts to communicate have failed.

■ Alex gets very annoyed with some of the language used by his business partner. For example, he calls their monthly meetings 'face time' and, when trying to arrange meetings, asks Alex when he can 'circle with' a supplier (i.e. meet with them).

■ Sometimes when Alex tries to use the mobile phone the signal is poor. This is particularly embarrassing when he is talking to a new customer for the plasma screen advertising because it gives a bad impression.

■ Evolution Barbers is considering franchising its business model and has created a booklet to explain the idea to potential franchisees. They asked friends to read the 50-page document and give them feedback; 'too long', 'boring', 'no pictures' and 'font too small' were some of the comments they received.

Activities

3 Prepare a PowerPoint presentation for Evolution Barbers explaining the barriers to communication they are experiencing.

4 Suggest two ways in which they could change what they currently do to improve communications. Make sure that you justify your suggestions.

AQA Examiner's tip

You should be able to explain the barriers that can prevent effective communication taking place, in a particular context.

7

In this chapter you have learnt:

✔ the purpose and importance of communication

✔ how to get a message across effectively

✔ choosing the right medium for communication

✔ barriers to communication.

Revision question

Match the terms on the left with the correct definition on the right.

Term		Definition	
1	Information	A	A business that has several layers of managers and supervisors from the top to the bottom.
2	Data	B	A way of communicating any information or data for any purpose.
3	Hierarchy	C	Written records of meetings for future reference.
4	Team	D	A specialist language for a particular group or industry which is unfamiliar to the general public.
5	Medium	E	A collection of words, pictures or numbers that has meaning in a given context.
6	Confidential	F	Details of what is to be discussed at a future meeting.
7	Minutes	G	A group of people working together to achieve a specific goal or target.
8	Agenda	H	Anything that disrupts the message as it is passed from the sender to the receiver.
9	Jargon	I	Facts and figures of any sort held by a business that can be processed to give information.
10	Noise	J	Information or data only available to people with authorised access.

Case study

Transglobe Communications plc

This multinational business has offices in major cities across the world. In the UK the company employs 500 staff at its head office in Bedford and 1,500 engineers throughout the country who work from home. The engineers repair and maintain business and home communications systems (telephone, broadband, television) and receive a daily schedule of jobs directly from Bedford. New and existing customers can contact the company through its call centre in India. In other countries Transglobe is involved in business-to-business operations providing communications solutions involving the latest technology.

Activities

1. Draw a diagram to illustrate how a fault in a home communications system in Preston, Lancashire, is communicated to the nearest engineer.

2. Explain the benefits to Transglobe of having well-informed engineers and happy UK customers.

3. Select the most suitable method of communication for the following circumstances:

   a. Call centre operators need new product training.

   b. A possible new business client in Australia wants to know about the products and services offered by Transglobe.

   c. Engineers are to be offered bonus payments for meeting new job completion targets.

   d. The Board of Directors wants details of sales figures for the past three years.

4. Using relevant examples, explain why communications between customers in the UK and overseas and Transglobe might go wrong.

8 ICT and business communications

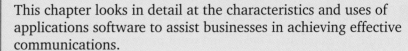

In this chapter

8.1 Word processing

8.2 Spreadsheets

8.3 Databases

8.4 Graphics and desktop publishing

8.5 Using local and wide area networks

This chapter looks in detail at the characteristics and uses of applications software to assist businesses in achieving effective communications.

Throughout this chapter reference will be made to the following case study, which forms the basis for the application of the information discussed.

Case study

Evolution Barbers

Alex Kamintzis wants to make as much use as possible of the computer and laptop he has bought, because he sees them as a good way to run his business efficiently. He thinks they will become even more valuable as the business expands and is considering the following areas of potential use:

- storing customer details including styling options and products purchased
- location details where Evolution Barbers currently operates
- storing details of suppliers Evolution Barbers uses
- keeping details of business customers that currently advertise on the plasma screen in his mobile salon
- recording stock and equipment purchases and sales: shampoos, conditioners, hair tonics and clippers
- save money by using publishing software to create his own advertising
- improve the presentation he has been asked to give to local school pupils.

8.1 Word processing

Uses of word-processing software

Before the development of the PC and **word processing**, a specialist, who was employed for his/her accuracy and speed at the typewriter, typed most documents used by businesses.

The development of word-processing software used on desktop and laptop computers has revolutionised the work of administrative staff within business and when communicating with stakeholders. Word-processed document files can easily be sent to colleagues and customers electronically by email or by other internet facilities.

Letterheads

In order to communicate information to clients about a business, a unique letterhead can be designed using word-processing software. This can help to create an image (e.g. traditional, modern or humorous) as well as give contact details.

Objectives

Understand the main features of word-processing software for use in a business.

Key terms

Word processing: using a dedicated application software to create, edit, format and print documents.

A *Written communication technology before the development of the word processor*

Activity

1 Using the examples shown on these pages as a guide, create a display showing how businesses in your area use word-processed documents to communicate. Select your favourite two examples and write an analysis of their contribution to the businesses communication.

a What information is included?

b How do the font style, size and colour help to create an image?

c Is a picture or graphic used and, if so, what does it add to the image created?

Envelopes and labels

External communications are very important to businesses, and a word-processing package can be used to change the look of a simple envelope. Special text and graphics, such as the company logo or a decorative graphic, can be added and applied to a wide range of envelope sizes. Labels for envelopes are useful for mass mailing

B *Business envelopes*

and can be created using an electronic address book. The labels can be previewed and the content rearranged. Here the advantage to the business is not only the time saved, but also the professional image that can be easily achieved.

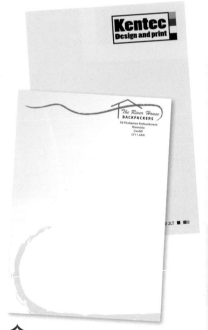

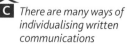

C *There are many ways of individualising written communications*

Business cards and flyers

Word-processing software can be used to create simple marketing documents such as business cards and flyers very cheaply and easily, although page layout software is more widely used because it often provides pre-designed templates to make the process easier, and it is more suited to commercial printing. As with letterheads, the use of font style and size, colour and pictures helps to create an image for the business as well as communicate information.

Standardised documents and mail merge

Word-processing software stores documents electronically so they can be printed when needed. Instead of writing a new letter for each customer or supplier, text can be stored as a standard letter and mail merge used to combine it with the relevant names and addresses. This saves the business a lot of time and reduces the likelihood of spelling and grammatical mistakes.

Formatting, inserts and borders

A 'house style' can be created using word-processing software, so all documents produced have the same format, font and layout. This makes everything look more professional. Additional material from a range of sources – such as spreadsheets, databases and graphics packages – can also be inserted into word-processed documents, and these can make the content clearer or more detailed. Sections of text that are particularly important can be highlighted with a box or border, for instance where a contract needs to be signed.

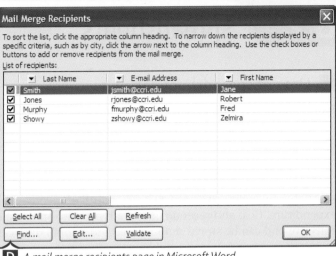

D *A mail merge recipients page in Microsoft Word*

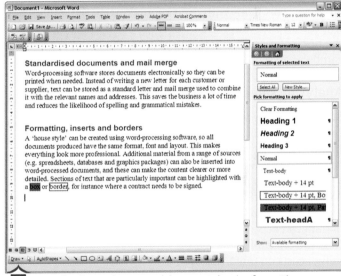

E *Example of a word-processed document showing formatting and borders to highlight text*

Evolution Barbers

Case study

Alex Kamintzis is now working full time at Evolution Barbers. He takes his mobile hairdressing salon to business parks around Watford and has set up a website **www.evolutionbarbers.co.uk** to pass on information to potential clients. However, Alex thinks that he could make more use of his computer, particularly the word-processing software.

Activity

2 Prepare a 500-word report advising Alex how he could use word-processing software to improve his business communications.

∞links

For details on page layout software, see pages 84–85.

AQA *Examiner's tip*

The content and look of the letter says a lot about the business, so the appropriate use of font style, size and accuracy is very important.

Spreadsheets

◼ Uses of spreadsheet software

Spreadsheet software packages are like big calculators that can hold a lot of data and sums for use over and over again. They contain many functions and features to help businesses make calculations.

Analysing financial data

All successful businesses need to keep control of income and expenditure. Cost and revenue data are typed into spreadsheet software and can be stored until needed. Additional data can be added at any time very easily and quickly, and adjustments made if necessary. The advantage of a spreadsheet is that the progress of the business can be tracked and information about its financial situation is available at all times. This helps with decision-making as the impact of changes to, say, the interest rate (a cost) or the price of a product (revenue) can be analysed.

Analysing sales

Business-specific spreadsheets can be used to forecast sales trends from past sales data stored in a firm's computer system. It is also possible to do 'What if?' scenarios in which the effect of a change to one piece of data can be seen on another (e.g. the effect of an increase in fuel costs on profit can be explored). This is particularly useful for marketing staff when they are deciding where to target resources. Sales figures can be analysed by customer, product or geographical region, for instance.

Key terms

Spreadsheet: software application in which the working area is divided into cells in rows and columns. Text and numbers are typed into the cells to be manipulated using formulae, and stored for future use.

			Current Year
	2004	2005	2006
Revenues	10,000	10,000	10,000
Cost of Goods Sold	4,000	4,000	4,000
Selling, general and administrative expenses	2,500	2,500	2,500
Depreciation	1,500	1,500	1,500
Amortisation of goodwill	0	0	0
Interest expense, net	1,000	1,000	1,000
Total costs and expenses	9,000	9,000	9,000
Provision for income taxes	(300)	(300)	(300)
Income before extraordinary items	700	700	700
Extrardinary items	0	0	0
Net income	700	700	700
Shares outstanding	10,000	10,000	10,000
Earnings per share (EPS) before extraordinary items	0.07	0.07	0.07
Earnings per share (EPS)	0.07	0.07	0.07
Dividends	(200)	(200)	(200)
Exercise of Stock Options	0	0	0
Shares issued	0	0	0
Foreign Currency Adjustment	0	0	0

A *A financial spreadsheet*

Analysing stock

At any time a business needs to know how much stock it has, for example the amount of raw materials or the number of components or finished goods waiting to be sold. Spreadsheet software can give the value of stock whenever needed, very quickly. It is also easy to find out which products are being sold quickly and which have been on the shelf too long, when stocks need to be re-ordered and how quickly an order can be delivered. All this information is important for business decision-making and for communicating with customers and suppliers.

B *How data can be displayed to help understanding*

Did you know ??????

The world's most used spreadsheet software is Microsoft Excel.

Paying wages and salaries

Staff wages and salaries, National Insurance contributions and tax can be calculated very quickly using a spreadsheet. Again, the biggest advantage over a paper-based system is the time saved, but there is also a huge benefit in terms of storing sensitive data securely as a single detailed record.

AQA *Examiner's tip*

You must be able to explain the benefits to a business of using a spreadsheet.

Displaying data

Once data has been entered onto a spreadsheet it can be sorted and displayed in several ways. It could be that the information is best presented in ascending order (e.g. the least profitable to the most profitable). On the other hand, data could be sorted alphabetically or in date order (chronologically). All these options are achieved very easily and quickly.

A spreadsheet can hold a huge amount of data, and it is very difficult to analyse its significance in its raw state. However, the software allows the data to be displayed in a variety of formats (e.g. graphs, charts and tables) that provide useful information. This means that more people are likely to understand the significance of the data e.g. sales trends or wage costs).

C *Sales analysis from a spreadsheet*

Evolution Barbers

Alex needs to keep track of his costs and revenue at Evolution Barbers. In particular he wants more information about the stocks of shampoo, conditioner and other hair care products he buys and sells. He uses branded products, which are quite expensive; however, he has found that clients want to buy the products he uses, so he believes it could be another source of income for the business. At the moment all his records are kept in a paper-based filing system, which is quickly filling up all the available space and he is not sure how much of his stock is for use in the salon and how much is sold to customers!

D *The interior of the Evolution Barbers salon*

8.3 Databases

Uses of databases

Details of customers, suppliers and sales were once written in ledgers and on paper stored in files like the ones you may use for your notes.

Computer software allows the electronic storage of a huge amount of data. Collecting data is a suitable format is called data capture. A **data-capture form** is used to collect the data in a user-friendly way. Each piece of data is stored in the **database** a **field** and when all the fields about a subject are put together they become a **record**.

Customer and supplier information

A database can help a business build up a profile of customers and group them according to similarities in particular fields. The business can then communicate with customers. It will also be possible to identify those that haven't bought anything for over a year who can be offered incentives to encourage them to purchase again. When compiling customer and supplier records, the use of data capture tools means that records should not be misspelled, contain incorrect data or miss important details.

Employee details

Having a detailed database about employees can help to improve communications within a business:

- Notices can be posted to individuals or groups of employees.
- Employees can download company documents (e.g. holiday forms).
- Personal information can be updated.
- Factors such as attendance, training, skills and employment history can be tracked.

Stock and equipment details

A database can be useful for logging details about stock and equipment used by a business so that:

- customer enquiries about the availability of products can be answered promptly
- service history, repairs and upgrades can be accessed quickly
- customers who have purchased faulty products can be contacted directly which may prevent accidents and maintain customer loyalty.

Sorting, searching, reporting and multiple users

A database gives a business the opportunity to make the best use of the data it holds. Restrictions are placed on access to sensitive data, however general data can be viewed in an appropriate form by more than one person at once. This saves time and improves reliability

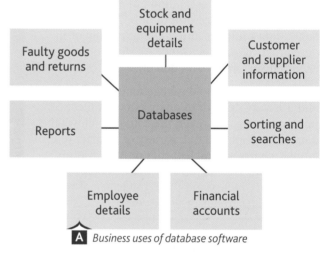

A Business uses of database software

(Diagram showing "Databases" in the centre connected to: Stock and equipment details, Customer and supplier information, Sorting and searches, Financial accounts, Employee details, Reports, Faulty goods and returns)

B A traditional paper-based filing system

because everybody is using the same data. Reports can be prepared using information gleaned from a database (e.g. the number of new workers employed in the last three months or the most common causes of products being returned).

Relational databases

A single data record can be useful for simple searches (e.g. customers who live in a particular area), but as a business grows in size, it may be necessary to create many types of records so that more complicated searches can be performed (e.g. customers in a specific area who bought a particular product and paid cash). A relational database identifies relationships between records based on common fields (e.g. a unique client reference code). In the example below, the dental practice can easily search for which of their NHS patients has had cosmetic dentistry.

A dental practice may create:

- records of all patients
- records of particular procedures (e.g. fillings, extractions)
- records of NHS patients
- records of private patients
- records of cosmetic dentistry patients.

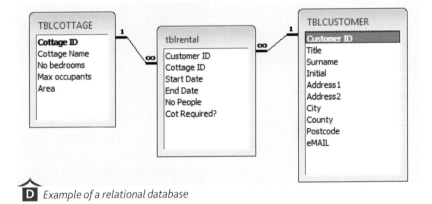

D Example of a relational database

C Storing information on a database of customers, suppliers or employees can reduce paperwork overload

Activity

1 Find out what sort of data is stored at your school or college. Is it stored on a database or in a paper-based filing system? What are the benefits of storing data in these ways?

AQA Examiner's tip

You must be able to describe the characteristics (features) of databases as well as the uses of databases.

∞ links

Remember that there are restrictions placed on all businesses about the data they can hold. See pages 46–47, Data protection and the law.

Evolution Barbers

Alex wants to make more use of his computer to run his business as efficiently as possible. He is keen to develop the database capability and is considering the following alternatives:

- lists of suppliers Evolution Barbers uses
- customer details including styling options and products purchased
- location details where Evolution Barbers currently operates
- details of business customers that currently advertise on the plasma screen in his mobile salon
- stock and equipment details (e.g. shampoos, conditioners, hair tonics, hair dryers and clippers).

Activity

2 You have been asked to advise Alex about which alternatives listed in the case study are suitable for storing on a database. You should explain why it would be of benefit to Evolution Barbers to use a database rather than a manual system for storing data. If you do not think a database is appropriate, you should explain why.

Case study

8.4 Graphics and desktop publishing

Uses of graphics software

Benefits of using graphics

- **Graphics** give a quick way for an audience to visualise what is being said during a presentation. This should mean that they will have a better understanding of the content. For example, aerial and ground-level photographs of a proposed location for a new retail outlet make it easier for the audience to appreciate the benefits of the site.

- They give a compact way to convey a lot of information. For example, an organisational structure, which would be very difficult to describe clearly and concisely just using text, can be shown as one diagram.

- They are more interesting than just speech or printed text. Images can provide clarity (e.g. to instruction leaflets). In other circumstances graphics provide welcome humour or visual stimulation to what might otherwise be a very dull document.

- They provide visual impact to ensure that a message being communicated is brought to the attention of the reader. This can be seen on advertising hoardings and magazine covers.

However, inappropriate and over use of graphics can distract the reader or audience from what might be an important business document or presentation, potentially losing customers.

Objectives

Understand the use of graphics and desktop publishing software.

Key terms

Graphic: any image (including diagrams, drawings, digital photographs and charts) made with the help of a computer.

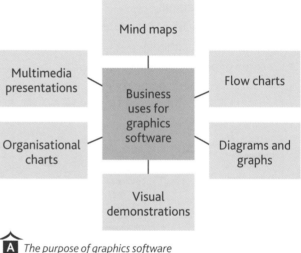

A *The purpose of graphics software*

Activity

1. Collect a range of examples of how businesses use graphics to help them communicate with customers. You can use company websites, advertisements in magazines and newspapers, and instructions provided with products either as part of the packaging or as additional information leaflets.

   As a class or in groups, discuss whether or not the graphics have been used effectively by the business to communicate information to the customer.

Did you know ??????

The Advertising Standards Agency (ASA) regulates the advertising industry and has forced companies to withdraw adverts that contain controversial graphics. To find out more visit **www.asa.org.uk**.

Uses of page layout software

There are many similarities between word-processing software and page layout software. The main difference is that word-processing software is primarily for text-based documents, whereas page layout software is specifically designed for specialised image and text placement, and gives output suitable for professional printing.

Did you know ??????

Page layout software used to be known as desktop publishing software.

Benefits of using page layout software

- Text and font size can be used to create a particular image for the business (e.g. contemporary or traditional). Specific details in a document can be highlighted to emphasise their importance.

- Graphics can be incorporated into a document to enhance the image the business wishes to create or to achieve visual impact.

- Price lists, catalogues and flyers can be updated easily and printed as required so they don't become out of date.

- In-house newsletters can be published that contain articles of interest to employees. This is a cheap and effective way of communicating information to employees.

- Professional business cards (that incorporate house style and the company logo) can be designed for all employees who need them.

B *The business uses of a page layout software package*

C *Catalogues are just one of the many business materials that can be produced with page layout software*

> **Remember**
>
> The graphics and desktop style must reflect the image of the business to be effective.

> AQA **Examiner's tip**
>
> Remember that the sort of graphics used should complement the business.

Evolution Barbers

Case study

Alex Kamintzis has some new projects coming up in the near future including:

- giving a presentation about his business to students at the local college

- preparing a report for his bank manager to show how the business has grown

- producing a quarterly newsletter for his clients

- updating his flyers and leaflets to give a more professional image.

> **Activity**
>
> 2   In small groups, prepare a five-minute presentation about the advantages to Alex of using graphics and page layout software.

D *Alex's Evolution Barbers salon*

Chapter 7 discussed the importance of communication within a business. ICT can be used to improve communication and share data within a business including:

- databases
- commonly used files
- software
- peripherals (e.g. printers).

Local area networks

Local area networks (LANs) link computers and peripherals in one location.

Types of LAN

Peer-to-peer

Here, two or more computers are connected directly so that employees doing the same kind of work can share applications and data. This system tends to be very slow, but it is robust as it does not rely on a central server which can fail.

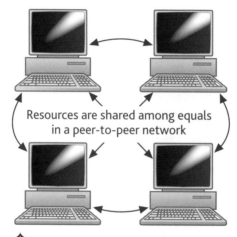

Resources are shared among equals in a peer-to-peer network

A *Peer-to-peer network configuration*

Client–server

Here, one powerful computer in the network acts as a server to all the others. The server computer holds all the application software and the shared files. All the files are stored centrally and users have the possibility of working on the same file at the same time.

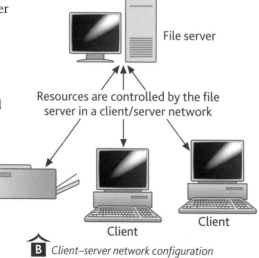

File server

Resources are controlled by the file server in a client/server network

Client

Client

B *Client–server network configuration*

⬯links

For more information, reread the purpose and importance of communication on pages 68–69.

Key terms

Local area network: a computer network set up for a single building or site.

Did you know ???????

The George Eliot NHS Trust Hospital in Nuneaton, Warwickshire, is putting in a Wireless LAN (WLAN). With the WLAN system, doctors, nurses and support staff will be able to electronically retrieve patient records from anywhere in the hospital.

■ Wide area networks

If a business operates in more than one location the need to share data and applications becomes even more important. **Wide area networks** (WANs) let users communicate efficiently between sites within one country and globally. WANs have the following features:

- They connect LANs.
- The networks are more complex.
- The WAN is based around central server computers.
- The central server computers are connected via a telecommunications network leased from businesses (e.g. British Telecom).

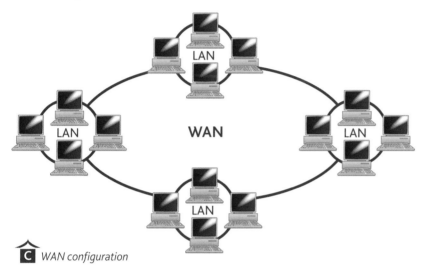

C *WAN configuration*

If a business decides to only share its network internally either using a LAN or a WAN, then this system is called an **intranet**.

If a business decides to open its network up to suppliers and customers, this is called an extranet and is usually accessed via a password.

Most businesses are connected to the internet via cable or broadband services. This is discussed in more detail in the next chapter.

Did you know ??????

Eighteen schools in the Bolton area of Lancashire have installed a broadband WAN. It provides the following facilities:

- A link to the main LEA core network.
- Video conferencing to facilitate lessons between schools.
- Resource sharing within the group of schools.
- An intranet with digital video content.

Did you know ??????

The BBC is known for its broadcast output and digital channels so you do not really think about the communication within the corporation. In fact, the BBC's intranet team are responsible for communications between its 29,000 production and support staff spread across the whole of the UK and abroad.

For more examples go to **www.simply-communicate.com** and search 'intranet'.

Evolution Barbers

Alex needs to link his home computer with the laptop he uses in the mobile hairdressing van. He knows that the benefits of this are a bit limited at the moment, but he hopes to expand his business in the near future and would need an intranet to share information.

Case study

Activities

2 Advise Alex about the best type of network for his needs.

3 Describe some of the uses he could make of a network to ensure good communications as his business grows.

Activity

1 Investigate your school's or college's intranet.

a Discuss its purpose.

b How and why is access restricted?

c How and why is use encouraged?

AQA *Examiner's tip*

WANs and LANs are not suitable for all businesses. You should be able to apply your knowledge appropriately.

Chapter summary

8

In this chapter you have learnt:

✔ the main features of word-processing software

✔ the uses of spreadsheet software

✔ the uses of a database

✔ the uses of graphics and desktop publishing software

✔ the features and uses of local and wide area networks.

Revision questions

Decide if the following statements are true or false.

1 Word processing prevents the creation of standard documents and increases the time spent entering text.

2 Word-processing software allows businesses to create their own letterheads without needing to use an external printing company.

3 A spreadsheet can be used to keep a record of sales revenue.

4 A disadvantage of spreadsheets is that the data entered can be altered and all other calculations resulting from one change are automatically changed.

5 Charts and graphs cannot be created from spreadsheets.

6 A database is a computer-based filing system.

7 Collecting data in a suitable format is called a relational database.

8 A data-capture form is a user-friendly way of collecting data to be stored on a database.

9 Text size and font style can be used to create an image and highlight details.

10 An intranet is a network shared between different businesses.

Case study

Transglobe Communications plc

As a communications company, Transglobe prides itself on using the latest technology to communicate with its customers, suppliers and employees. The company intranet system has been running for many years and is regularly updated to ensure that data can be shared as efficiently as possible. At the moment, the IT department is developing an extranet to be trialled next year for business customers in the UK. Transglobe uses relational databases to track particular problems that occur with installations and this has resulted in a reduction in the number of faults. Desktop publishing software was used to create easy-to-follow instructions for customers who had complained that the support manuals were too difficult to read.

Activities

1 Explain the features of an intranet.

2 Explain the main features of a relational database and the restrictions placed on a business about the data they can hold.

3 Explain how the use of desktop publishing can help Transglobe create a customer-friendly image.

9 The internet and e-commerce

In this chapter

9.1   The purpose of a website

9.2   Opportunities provided by having a website

9.3   Risks in using the internet

The business environment is increasingly competitive and those businesses that can respond positively to potential and actual competition are likely to be the most successful. The internet can help with this as it provides many opportunities to bring buyers and sellers together, to pass on and collect valuable information about goods and services.

Chapter 9.1 considers the range of reasons for having a website. The ways in which businesses use the internet are identified, described and evaluated. This includes telling customers about the business and its products, as well as the creation of an internet shop enabling customers to order and pay for goods and services online.

Chapter 9.2 is concerned with the business opportunities presented by the internet and e-commerce. This includes the possibility of increasing, or at least maintaining, the share of an existing market by operating a 24/7 online service.

Chapter 9.3 considers the risks to businesses of the internet and e-commerce. The disadvantages include the threats of increased competition, the costs of establishing and maintaining a website, and the risks of unauthorised access and theft of customer data.

Case study

Evolution Barbers

Evolution Barbers uses the internet in order to promote the business as widely as possible. Alex has already started developing a website but wants to make better use of the opportunities offered by the world wide web. He has been looking at other hairdressers' websites for inspiration: oojufink. com; g-dhairsalon.co.uk; richardnorman.co.uk; Gents.co.uk.

Alex's own Evolution Barbers website uses the following pages:

- Homepage with a video link to the BBC Working Lunch feature.
- Services: typical salon hairdressing with prices.
- Appointments: where the van will be each day.
- About us: a bit of background about Alex and the business.
- Contact us: a telephone number and e-mail address for questions and feedback.

Did you know ??????

Online has become the most important channel of distribution for mail-order retailers. Online ordering generated nearly 41 per cent of all sales in this £9.9 billion market in 2007.

Source: www.just-style.com

Did you know ??????

More than seven out of ten internet users have made a purchase online. It is a safe and convenient way to shop as the incidence of computer hackers stealing and using cardholder data is very low.

Source: www.dcs.napier.as.uk

What is the internet?

The **internet** is a worldwide system linking single computers and networks together using software and cables. There isn't a headquarters for the internet; it is maintained by network administrators all over the world. To access the world wide web to view particular **websites**, we use a web **browser** (e.g. Microsoft Internet Explorer, Mozilla Firefox or Safari).

A *The home page for Game, an online retailer of console games*

Caution

Although the internet gives access to a huge source of information, it should always be treated with caution. In the UK there are laws to protect consumers from untrue or misleading advertisements (e.g. the Sale of Goods Acts), however it is very difficult to control what is posted on the internet.

Use of search engines

The main problem facing users of the internet is how to find what they are looking for from the millions of websites and billions of web pages. Search engines (e.g. Google and Ask) act like huge databases and allow searches either by keywords or phrases, or by answering a question (a concept search). It is very important for businesses to make sure that their website is on the database of the most popular search engines, and that through the index of keywords their website appears when potential customers do a search.

The growth of the internet happened because businesses realised the potential to:

- sell to and buy from other businesses around the world (this is called 'business to business')
- sell directly to consumers around the world.

The development of interactive websites links suppliers and customers electronically.

Key terms

Internet: a global system linking individual computers and computer networks together.

Website: a related collection of web pages linked by a home page.

Browser: software that allows the user to view content on the internet or the world wide web.

Did you know ??????

Wikipedia is the biggest multinational free content encyclopaedia in the world; volunteers around the world have written it and the vast majority of its articles can be edited/changed by anyone with access to the internet.

Did you know ??????

In the first half of 2008, nearly 20 per cent of spending by UK shoppers was done online.

Source: www.bbc.co.uk

Did you know ??????

eBay UK was launched in October 1999 and has over 14 million active users. eBay estimates that 178,000 users run a business or use eBay as their primary or secondary source of income.

Source: www.eBay.co.uk

Uses of the internet and websites

E-commerce has seen spectacular growth over the past ten years. It includes retailing, auctions, music downloads, service providers, the government and business to business.

Activity

1 Match the purposes of e-commerce on the left to the examples of websites on the right.

1	Retailing	A	www.confused.com
2	Auctions	B	www.vehiclelicence.gov.uk
3	Music downloads	C	www.argos.co.uk
4	Service providers	D	www.eBay.co.uk
5	The government	E	www.napster.co.uk

Online catalogue

An **online catalogue** is a list of items a business sells, usually with a description (including precise details) and price. There is sometimes a greater range of products available online than 'over the counter' in a traditional retail outlet.

∞**links**

For further information about online recruitment go to pages 52–53, How to recruit the right person for the job.

E-commerce

This takes the online catalogue one step further and allows customers to choose and pay for items. Websites usually create an e-mail confirmation of an order and it is possible to track an order to delivery. Returns can also be arranged online.

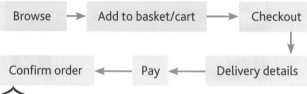

B *The online ordering process*

Information provider

As part of customer service, many businesses now provide online information including:

- details of the company history, future plans and financial performance
- news – product launches, awards and press releases
- charities – support given by the business to particular good causes
- ethics – the company's policies on the environment, fair trade and responsible business practices
- product information – user manuals and specifications.

Method of recruitment

More and more businesses aim to fill vacancies by advertising on their website. Other firms use dedicated recruitment sites, which advertise jobs for a wide range of employers. Many are industry-specific or relate to a particular geographical area.

Activities

2 Explain the advantage of recruiting a new stylist for Evolution Barbers through the website.

3 Alex is considering selling hair care and grooming products to his clients. Evaluate the ways in which he could use the website for this new service.

4 Alex realises that more and more barbers are improving the service they offer (see **www.jacksoflondon.com**, for example). Discuss how he can use the internet to respond to potential competition from other barbers.

It is now possible for businesses of all types and sizes to have a website that enables customers to buy online. Here are the main features of an e-commerce website that helps a business communicate better with customers.

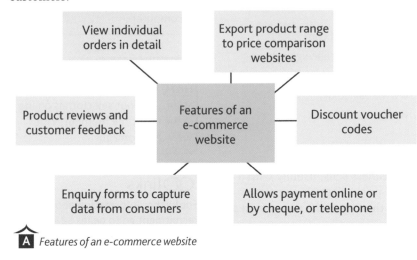

A *Features of an e-commerce website*

Objectives

Understand the business opportunities offered by the internet and e-commerce.

Understand how the internet can help businesses respond to competition.

Activity

1 Sketch an e-commerce web page for a company 'CoolSkool' that specialises in selling school equipment (e.g. pencil cases and school bags) to fashion-conscious teenagers. Use **www.goprojectors.co.uk** as a guide to content and format.

Trading round the clock

With a website a business can communicate with customers 24/7; taking orders does not need employees or even a building, and customers can buy at a time that suits them. This will help the business manage its orders better than a firm that is only open for limited hours, where queues and delays could be more of a problem.

Protecting market share

In a competitive market, it is important to protect market share. Investing in a website might be expensive in the short term, but can strengthen a businesses position in the longer term.

- An online catalogue and ordering service reduces costs (e.g. wages, premises, stationery and printing).
- Communicating with customers via the internet is quicker and more efficient than by non-electronic means. Orders can be tracked, visitors to a website can be asked specific questions, customer feedback can be used for product reviews and discount voucher codes may encourage loyalty.

B *Goprojectors' home page*

Getting information about competitors

Businesses need to know what their competitors are doing. By looking at the websites of the **competition** a firm can see what products are on offer and the sorts of promotional strategies being used (e.g. buy one, get one free).

Key terms

Competition: other businesses operating in a market.

Reaching customers

Close to one billion people around the world have internet access and this means that a business should be able to reach its target market and get them to look at what it has to offer.

Providing customer care

Marketing is about meeting the needs of consumers. Firms need to make sure that they know what it is that their customers really want so that they become loyal to the brand or business. Having a questionnaire or comments page on a website makes it easier to provide the service customers want. This could include posting special offers and providing online technical support.

Summary

By using the internet a business can become more competitive. Giving customers access to products 24/7 could lead to an increase in market share. Information about company activities can help to encourage customer loyalty. Encouraging online feedback can help a business to improve quality. The most successful businesses will use the internet to identify and respond to potential and actual competition and ensure that they maintain or improve their market position.

Did you know ??????

Portalspace Records began in 2001 making vinyl records and has established itself as a leading manufacturer of quality record pressings. Everything and everyone at the company is dedicated to the provision of a fast, consistent and reliable supply to meet the customers' needs. For further details go to **www.portalspacerecords.com**.

Case study

Evolution Barbers

When Alex first set up Evolution Barbers, one problem he faced was how to get his business known to potential clients on the industrial estates around Watford. One option was to print flyers giving details of where the mobile salon would be each day and the prices Alex charged. However, although this option is quite cheap, there was a good chance that the potential clients would just think of it as junk mail and throw it away. It would also make it difficult for Alex to change any of the details without having to print new flyers.

Alex was also very keen to get feedback from his clients so that he could improve the service he provided to better meet the needs of his customers. He found that most people were polite when he asked about the quality of a haircut and very few completed the questionnaire he put in the salon.

Thirdly, Alex wanted to be sure that his prices were competitive. He knew that his target customer was the man with a strong concern for his appearance, and who spent a lot of time and money on his image and lifestyle. Alex did not have time to visit all the competition in the Watford area and, even after asking friends, was not convinced that his prices were competitive.

Activities

3   How can a website be used to solve the problems Alex faces with promoting the business?

4   Design a short online feedback form that Alex could use to find out how to improve the service he offers.

5   How could Alex use the internet to find out competitive prices to charge?

Activity

2   Ania, a Polish restaurant in Nottingham, is very popular and always busy. At the moment the business does not have its own website, but can be found at **www.nottingham-restaurants.co.uk**. This site gives basic information about opening times, the menu and wine list with prices. It also has photographs of the premises.

Write a letter to the owner of Ania, Mrs Kisielowski, outlining the benefits of creating a website specifically for her business.

9.3 Risks in using the internet

Although there are many advantages to setting up a website for a business, there are also problems that must be considered.

◼ Security threats

A security breach usually results in a serious disruption to business. Today **hackers** are writing extremely powerful hacking tools to gain unauthorised access to computers. Businesses often need to collect personal information about customers using their website. It is very important that the data is secure as customers need to be reassured that their privacy is protected. **Secure Sockets Layer (SSL)** is an industry standard used by millions of websites to protect online transactions. In order to be able to generate an SSL link, a web server requires SSL certification (shown by a padlock image on the web browser).

A

Threats	Prevention
Unauthorised access to sensitive data, including customers' bank details, by hackers who may view, alter or destroy private files. Denial of service (DoS) attack in which hackers disable a network and stop the business operating online.	Data encryption works by encoding the text of a message with a key. Standard security technology creates an encrypted link between a web server and a browser. This ensures that all online data remains private and integral.
Payment protection is a necessity for a business wishing to trade online because the trust of the consumer is vital.	Secure Electronic Transactions mean that the minimum amount of information necessary is given to the business.
Viruses are destructive programs that attach themselves to e-mail, applications and files. Users can quickly damage entire networks by downloading and launching viruses.	Firewalls provide a single point through which all traffic to and from the internet must pass and are an organisation's first line of defence against Internet intruders.
Private data hackers using programs called 'packet sniffers' can capture data as it passes over the internet.	Virus protection is often included as part of the package offered by a web-hosting company.

◼ Cost of setting up and maintaining site

There are a large number of start-up costs (e.g. for a domain name, full web hosting and email facilities, design fees, upload to the server and submission to the major search engines). If the website is for selling products there will be maintenance costs such as updating the catalogue, stock control, tracking orders and customer communications, although the monthly costs may not be high. Costs depend on the level of service the business decides to offer.

◼ Threat of increased competition

Developing a website gives a business access to potential customers who might only find out about the company through a search engine. However, it also means that potential customers will be aware of all the competitors in the market. This means that a business will have to have a very effective website to attract customers.

Objective

Understand the disadvantages of the internet and e-commerce to a business.

Key terms

Hacker: a person gaining unauthorised access to a computer.

Secure Sockets Layer (SSL): the standard security technology for creating an encrypted link between a web server and a browser.

Payment protection: a way to buy or sell online securely.

B *Data security on a web browser is indicated by the padlock symbol*

Did you know ??????

UK businesses must abide by rules laid down in the Data Protection Act (**www.ico.gov.uk**).

Did you know ??????

Here is a copy of the QVC shopping channel's privacy statement:

'At QVC your privacy is a priority.

QVC does not sell or exchange customer information with anyone else. We share relevant information only with those parties entrusted with the processing of your account and the fulfilment of your order and to parties entrusted by us to undertake customer surveys. We have established procedures to protect your privacy – and we uphold them vigorously.'

■ Customer support outside office hours

It is very difficult to offer online customers any more out-of-hours support than a business with no website. There might be a 'frequently asked questions' page to assist customers, but the lack of personal support can cause frustration. To solve this problem some firms use 24/7 call centres, which will increase costs.

■ Consumers' buying habits

The description of the products must be very accurate when selling online because it is harder for the customer to buy an item when they cannot physically see it in front of them, especially for items where the measurements are important. Consumers are hesitant to buy some products online. Furniture businesses, for example, struggle because customers want to test the comfort of an expensive item such as a sofa before they buy it. Many people also consider shopping a social experience with friends or family, an experience that they cannot get online.

C *Two ways of shopping*

D *First Direct call centre*

Activity

1   Jacqui's Catering Service is available for celebration parties, family occasions and special events. At the moment Jacqui advertises in local newspapers and community magazines, but one of her clients suggested that she should have a website because it was very difficult to contact her for a quote.

Create a leaflet for Jacqui about implementing a website for customers to browse and order her catering services. Cover all the main advantages and disadvantages she can expect.

Evolution Barbers

Evolution Barbers may develop its existing website so that it can sell hair care and grooming products. However there are problems with this approach, such as the cost of setting up and maintaining the online shop and preventing unauthorised access to customer data.

Case study

Activities

2   List the possible drawbacks that Evolution Barbers could face if it develops the website to include an online shop.

3   How can he reassure customers who are concerned about buying products online?

4   In your opinion, would it be a good idea for Alex to introduce an online shop or should he develop his business in other ways (e.g. take the mobile salon to weddings, festivals and other big outdoor events)?

AQA *Examiner's tip*

Web selling is not suitable for all businesses. Understand when it will be most beneficial.

In this chapter you have learnt:

✔ the business use of the internet and websites

✔ the purposes of having a website

✔ the opportunities that having a website can bring

✔ the drawbacks of operating a website and e-commerce.

Revision questions

Match the terms with the correct definitions.

Term		Definition
1	E-commerce	A	A related collection of web pages linked by a home page.
2	Internet	B	A list of products stocked or manufactured by a business.
3	Website	C	Identifying, anticipating and satisfying consumer needs.
4	Browser	D	Any transaction involving the transfer of information over the internet.
5	Online catalogue	E	The percentage of a market accounted for by one brand or business.
6	Marketing	F	Businesses operating in a market.
7	Market share	G	A way to buy or sell online securely without sharing financial details.
8	Competition	H	A website that is certified as able to accept payment and other sensitive information securely.
9	Secure site	I	A global system linking individual computers and computer networks together.
10	PayPal	J	Software that allows the user to view content on the internet or the world wide web (e.g. Microsoft Internet Explorer).

Case study

Transglobe Communications plc

Transglobe has a very large and detailed website that provides a lot of information for stakeholders in the organisation. For customers there are product details and user manuals to support the equipment that is installed in the home. There is also a frequently-asked-question section to reduce the need for the engineer to visit. Transglobe also uses the website for its graduate recruitment programme, giving details of opportunities within the company and case studies of successful applicants. The company believes that the website is very important because it gives it an advantage over the competition and has helped it increase its market share. In particular, the managing director is pleased with the comments page which provides customer feedback. This has enabled the company to meet the needs of clients more effectively.

Activities

1 Explain why the internet is an important part of Transglobe's system of communication.

2 Identify and explain two opportunities that have been provided for Transglobe by having a website.

3 Explain the possible risks to Transglobe of operating a website in a very competitive market.

AQA | Examination-style questions

■ Examination skills Unit 8

This examination will assess three different skills.

Assessment Objective 1 assesses your knowledge and understanding of the concepts and terms in this unit. Questions that start with these words – 'state', 'list', 'give an advantage' or 'give a disadvantage' – will test this assessment objective.

Assessment Objective 2 assesses how you apply these concepts and terms to a specific business or task. Questions that ask you to 'explain' will test this assessment objective.

Assessment Objective 3 assesses how you can analyse a situation, make a reasoned judgement and present a conclusion. Questions that say 'justify', 'recommend' or 'decide' are testing this assessment objective. Your communications skills are also assessed in these questions.

The Unit 8 examination is a one-hour paper and the same paper is taken by all candidates. There is no foundation or higher tier. There are 60 marks on the paper and these are earned fairly evenly over the three assessment objectives. This means that it is just as important to be able to apply what you have learned to a specific business or task and draw a conclusion, as it is to learn the terms and concepts.

The examination will use one business case study throughout the paper, and will be split into three to four main sections. These sections will have a mixture of short and longer questions. In each section, there will be one question where you will be asked to analyse a situation and draw a conclusion.

Examination-style questions with model answers

Sue and Raj run a small greengrocery shop called 'Eat Your Greens', which they set up five years ago. The shop is on a busy high street next to other small shops. Before this, Sue worked as an assistant in a local supermarket and Raj sold cars at a local garage. Sue is responsible for dealing with the local farmers who supply them with most of their goods. This means that she is often out of the shop. Raj deals with the routine administrative tasks as well as serving in the shop. No other people work within the business. Both hope that the shop will be the first of a chain.

1   (a) State two objectives Sue and Raj may have for Eat Your Greens.   *(2 marks)*

> 1   To make as much profit as possible.
> 2   To make the business bigger and have another branch.

 Examiner's tip   Both of these answers are good and earn full marks.

(b) Sue and Raj are stakeholders in this business. State two other groups who may be stakeholders in this business. *(2 marks)*

1   Other local businesses.

2   Local people.

 Examiner's tip Both of these answers are correct. If the candidate has said 'employees', that would not be correct here because, at the moment, there are no other employees. So the answer must apply to this business.

As the shop has become busier, Sue and Raj decide that they will need to employ an assistant to work in the shop. They have decided that the person they employ should have the following skills:

Essential skills:
- experience of shop work
- good communication skills
- able to take responsibility if Sue and Raj both need to go out.

Desirable skills:
- able to use a computer
- an interest in food and cooking.

(c) State and explain three ways that Sue and Raj could advertise this new job. *(6 marks)*

1   A card in their shop window. This is a good idea as a shopper might just want a job and they will be local to the shop.

2   Advertise in the local newspaper. This is a good idea because more people will see the job and only local people will want the job.

3   In a Job Centre. More people will see the advert and they are all the people who are looking for a job.

 Examiner's tip These are all good, relevant suggestions with a good explanation, so would get full marks; 1 mark for each appropriate method and one mark for the explanation of each method. If a candidate had suggested a national newspaper or a website, these would be less good answers as these methods would not be the best in this situation.

Mark scheme for 1(c)

Level	Descriptor	Marks	Assessment Objective
2	Candidate explains why each method is suitable in this case.	4–6	AO2
1	Candidate identifies up to three relevant ways of advertising the job.	1–3	AO1

Sue and Raj advertise the job in the shop window and three people apply. Here are details from their applications.

Name	Qualifications	Experience	Hobbies
Mary	None	Worked in various local shops in the town for over 20 years	Reading, cooking, playing cards
Jim	5 GCSEs including maths and English	2 years' experience at a DIY store	Renovating cars, playing football
Milly	2 GCSEs, one is English	5 years' experience of shop work. Assistant manager at the local fish shop for the past year	Art, music, eating out

(d) Using the information above, explain how suitable each candidate would be for the post of assistant. Recommend which you think might be the best candidates to call for an interview. *(9 marks)*

> Mary has no qualifications but she has a lot of shop work experience, so she might be good. She also likes cooking which would be good in a shop that sells food.
>
> Jim has a GCSE in English which might mean that he is good at communicating, and he has worked in a shop. The shop is DIY not food, so he might not be the best person for a greengrocery shop.
>
> Milly does not have as many qualifications as Jim, but she has better experience and she has had a job as an assistant manager. I think that Milly might be the best person for the job because she matches the essential skills better than the other two. None of them can use a computer. I would interview Mary and Milly as they both sound like they might be good.

This is a very good answer and would gain full marks. The candidate has stated and explained the reason why they would interview Mary and Milly. The candidate has also looked at each person's strengths and weaknesses in a structured way. They have made a decision about which people to interview and given reasons for that decision. This shows very good judgement. The candidate has also used terms like, 'qualifications', 'work experience' and 'skills' appropriately.

Mark scheme for 1(d)

Level	Descriptor	Marks	Assessment Objective
1	Candidate explains why any of the three may be best to interview.	1	AO2
	Candidate states why any of the three may be best to interview.	1	AO1

Assessment Objective AO3 also assesses the quality of written communication skills.

Level	Descriptor	Marks	Assessment Objective
3	Candidate offers judgement of who to interview with justification. Ideas are communicated with a clear structure and use of appropriate terms from this part of the specification.	6–7	
2	Candidate offers judgement of who to interview with some justification. Ideas are communicated with some structure and use of appropriate terms from this part of the specification. There are occasional errors in spelling and grammar.	3–5	AO3
1	Candidate offers an unsupported judgement as to which candidates(s) to interview. Ideas are communicated in a simplistic way and there are errors in spelling and grammar.	1–2	

More examination-style questions

Going Away is a small travel agency. In the past, it mostly sold package holidays. However, sales have been falling steadily. Many people now want to put their own holiday together. They use a travel agent to find and book flights, hotels and visits from different tour operators.

Laura Andrews has recently bought the business. She believes that she can make the business successful. She wants to increase sales by offering a high level of personal service. This will also need far greater use of ICT to store, process and retrieve the huge amount of information used. Laura will need to buy new office furniture to improve the comfort of the staff, as much of their time is spent at the computer.

There are five full-time travel consultants who serve customers.

1   (a)   State two ways that Laura could measure the success of Going Away.   *(2 marks)*

       (b)   List two examples of data that may be stored on Going Away's computer system.   *(2 marks)*

       (c)   Explain why it is important that data stored in this computer system can be easily retrieved.   *(4 marks)*

       (d)   The business holds data about customers in the computer system. Describe two ways in which the Data Protection Act affects how they collect and use this data.   *(4 marks)*

       (e)   Laura needs to buy five new chairs that will be suitable for her workers. She has a brochure with three possible chairs. Recommend which one she should buy. Give reasons for your answer.   *(9 marks)*

Henley executive chair
Product no: 12790BK

- Traditional manager's chair
- Hardwood construction with top quality Italian leather seat and back rest
- Rocking and locking mechanism with weight tension control
- Pneumatic height adjuster
- Complete with sturdy fixed arms

PRICE £250

Adept contract task chair (fixed arms)
Product no: 24852BL

- Generously proportioned square back and seat for comfort and support
- Fixed loop arms
- Features gas height, synchronised mechanism, back height, back tilt and side tension adjustment
- Overall height 103cm
- Black nylon high centre 5-star base with oversize castors

PRICE £150

Identity operator chair
Product no: 24845RD

- High back 3-lever operator chair
- Generously proportioned back and seat for comfort and support
- Provides gas height, back angle and seat tilt adjustment
- Seat slide and ratchet back height adjustment
- Black nylon 5-star base with easy-glide castors

PRICE £100

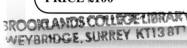

Laura likes to have a quick briefing meeting with her staff every morning for 10 minutes before the agency opens. She talks to them about any new developments that they need to know about, such as changes to prices of flights or special offers. Every month, a staff meeting takes place after work from 5.30pm to 6.30pm. During this meeting Laura tells the staff about which flights, hotels and trips are selling well and which they need to sell more of. There is also a notice board in the staff kitchen which is used for various sorts of communication. The staff can also e-mail each other at work.

2   (a) State two examples of communication that could be placed on the staff notice board.   *(2 marks)*

One member of staff has put up a notice advertising a car she is selling. Laura has asked her to take it down.

      (b) Explain why you think Laura may have done this.   *(2 marks)*

      (c) The staff use e-mail a lot. Explain two benefits of using it in this sort of business.   *(5 marks)*

The staff do not enjoy the after-work meeting as Laura talks for most of the time. They find it quite hard to remember all the information she tells them. A member of staff suggests to Laura that she uses a PowerPoint presentation and a projector to improve the way she communicates at these meetings.

      (d) Laura is not sure about spending money on this equipment. Recommend if she should use presentation software to make the meetings more useful for the staff? Give your reasons.   *(9 marks)*

Going Away has a website where customers can book their own flights and trips, rather than come into the agency themselves. More of their business is being done in this way. Some of the staff worry that this will make their job redundant in the future. Laura believes that some customers will always want to come in to the agency, rather than use the website.

3   (a) State two advantages for Going Away of having a website.   *(2 marks)*

      (b) Explain three reasons why some customers will not book their own holiday on a website.   *(6 marks)*

Laura is keen to make the website bigger and better for customers to use. Some of the staff think this means that they will lose their jobs.

Laura is going to hold a special meeting about the development of the website.

      (c) List three things she should consider when planning this meeting to make sure it runs smoothly.   *(3 marks)*

      (d) Do you think that Laura is right to keep developing the website side of the business? Give reasons for your answer.   *(9 marks)*

Index

Key terms are in blue

A

administration 16
  business functions 18–19
  data 16–17
  planning and prioritising 22–23
  roles and responsibilities 20–21
advertisements 73
Advertising Standards Agency
  (ASA) 84
age discrimination 57
agenda 72
aims 8
applications, job 55
authorised access 45
authority 20

B

bonuses 62
browsers 90
business cards 79, 85

C

call centres 27
carbon neutral businesses 36
cash flow 11
CDs (compact discs) 42
cellular offices 26–27
channels of communication
  70–71, 74
client-server networks 86
commission 62
communication
  barriers to 74–75
  benefits of effective 69
  ICT and 78–87
  importance 69
  mediums 70, 72–73, 74
  purpose 68
  systems 70–71
competition 92, 94

computers
  ergonomics and using 29
  see also ICT
confidential information 70
contracts of employment 50–51
creativity and working
  environment 27
curricula vitae (CVs) 55
customer services 18–19
customers
  communication and 69
  databases and 82
  internet and 93, 95
  as stakeholders 12

D

data 16
  input devices 40, 41
  output devices 42–43
  preparation 16
  processing 17
  protection 44–47
  retrieval 17
  sources 40–41
  spreadsheets and 80–81
  storage 16–17, 42, 82–83
Data Protection Act (1998) 46–47
data-capture forms 82
databases 82–83
decisions, routine and non-routine
  20–21
desks 28
desktop publishing software 84–85
digital cameras 41
Disability Discrimination Act 57
discrimination 56
display screen regulations 30
dissemination of data 17
DVDs (digital versatile discs) 42

E

e-commerce 91, 92–93
e-mail 73

efficiency 27
electricity, saving 37
electronic notice boards 72
employees
  communication and 69, 85
  contracts of employment 50–51
  details on databases 82
  employment rights 56–57
  and flexible working 35
  health and safety 30–31
  paying 62–63
  recruitment 52–53, 91
  rewards 64–65
  selection 54–55
  as stakeholders 12
  training 60–61
employers
  health and safety responsibilities
  30
employment equality (age)
  regulations 57
encryption 44
envelopes and labels 78
environment, business
  business aims and objectives
  8–9
  stakeholders 12–13
  successful businesses 10–11
environmentally friendly
  practices 13, 36, 37
equal opportunities 56
Equal Pay Act 56
ergonomics 28–29
ethics 11
external communications 68, 78
external recruitment 52–53
external training 60–61

F

fax messages 73
fields, database 82
finance function 18
financial data, analysing 80

financial documents 73
firewalls 44
flat business structures 20
flexi-time 34
flexible working 34–35
flow charts 73
flyers 79, 85
formal communications 70
fringe benefits 64
fuel, saving 37
full-time contracts 50
functions, business 18–19

G

government and businesses 12
graphics
    and communication 73
    software 84–85
growth 9, 10

H

hackers 44, 94
hard disks 42
health and safety 30–31
Health and Safety at Work Act 30
hierarchies in businesses 20
home working 34
hot desking 32
'house styles' 79
human resources (HR) 18

I

ICT
    databases 82–83
    graphics and desktop publishing
      84–85
    local and wide area networks
      86–87
    spreadsheets 80–81
    word processing 78–79
image 9
in-house training 60
induction training 60
informal communications 70
information 68
Information Commissioner 46

input devices, data 40–41
internal communication 68
internal recruitment 52
internet 90
    opportunities for business 92–93
    risks in using 94–95
    uses of 91
intranets 87

J

jargon 74
job creation 11
job descriptions 54
job sharing 35

K

keyboards 41

L

legislation 13
    data protection 46–47
    employment 56–57
    health and safety 30
letterheads 78
letters 73
local area networks (LANs) 86
local communities 12

M

mail merge 79
managers 20–21, 64
market share 10, 92
marketing 18
mediums of communication 70,
    72–73, 74
meetings 72
memos 73
minutes 72
monitors 42
mouse 41

N

National Minimum Wage 56
'noise' and communication 74
non-routine decisions 20–21

non-routine tasks 21
notice boards, electronic 72

O

objectives 8–9, 10
off-the-job training 60–61
online catalogues 91
open-plan offices 26
operations 18, 19
operatives 21
optical mark recognition (OMR) 41
oral communications 72
output devices, data 42–43
overtime 62
owners 12

P

paper, saving 37
part-time contracts 50
passwords 45
payment protection 94
peer-to-peer networks 86
permanent contracts 50
person specifications 54
plans 22–23
PowerPoint presentations 72, 75
primary data 40
printers 37, 43
prioritisation of tasks 23
production drawings 73
profitability 10
profits 8, 9, 10
projectors 43

Q

questionnaires 40

R

Race Relations Act 56
records, database 82, 83
recruitment of staff 52–53, 91
recruitment agencies 53
recycling 37
regulations 30
relational databases 83

reputation 9

research and development (R&D) 18, 19

resources, using with consideration 36–37

responsibility 20

rewards for employees 64–65

roles and responsibilities in businesses 20–21

routine decisions 21

routine tasks 21

S

salaries 62, 81

sales 18

  analysing 80

scanners 41

search engines 90

seasonal work 35

seats 28

secondary data 40

Secure Sockets Layer (SSL) 94

Sex Discrimination Act 56

shareholders 12

shift work 35

spreadsheets 80–81

staff *see* employees

stakeholders 12

stock

analysing 80

  details of 82–83

storage devices, data 42

structures, business 20–21

success, measuring 10–11

supervisors 20, 21

suppliers

  communication and 69

  databases and 82

sustainability 13, 36

T

targets 8–9

tasks, routine and non-routine 21

teams 27, 68

teleconferencing 32

telephone calls 72

teleworking 34

temporary contracts 50

text messages 73

trade unions 12

training for employees 60–61

U

unauthorised access 44, 45

urgent communications 71

USB (Universal Serial Bus) Memory Sticks 42

V

video conferencing 33

viruses 44–45

visual communications 72

voice recognition systems 41

W

wages 62, 81

webcams 41

websites 90

  opportunities for business 92–93

  problems 94–95

  uses of 91

wide area networks (WANs) 87

wireless networks 44, 45

word processing 78–79

workplaces

  effective design 28–29

  flexible working 34–35

  health and safety 30–31

  modern work practices 32–33

  using resources 36–37

  working environment 26–27

workstations 29

written communications 73